The

Old Catholic
CHURCH

*Understanding the Origin, Essence,
and Theology of a Church that is Unknown
and Misunderstood by Many in North America*

Robert W. Caruso

the apocryphile press
BERKELEY, CA
www.apocryphile.org

*This book is dedicated to those Catholic theologians
like Josef Ignaz von Döllinger and Pére Hyacinth
who sacrificed much for the glory
of Christ's Church on earth.*

Apocryphile Press
1700 Shattuck Ave #81
Berkeley, CA 94709
www.apocryphile.org

Printed in the United States of America
ISBN 1-933993-67-7

Table of Contents

Acknowledgements

THIS BOOK HAS BEEN A WORK in progress for the past three and a half years in conjunction with completing coursework for my Master of Divinity degree at United Theological Seminary. I have benefited greatly from the criticisms, debates and comments of my colleagues and friends alike. Their challenging questions and ideas helped me in producing this final text. I would like to also thank Paul E. Capetz, professor of Church History at United Theological Seminary. I am indebted to Dr. Capetz for his theological expertise, editing critiques and comments on Chapter One of my book. Thank you!

A special word of thanks to Rev. Bjorn Marcussen, Episcopal priest and Old Catholic theologian, for writing the introduction, as well as previewing my manuscript and providing me with helpful comments concerning its content. Fr. Marcussen's dedication to promoting the eucharistic ecclesiology of the local-universal church is apparent and his wisdom is appreciated.

I am grateful to the Cornerstone Old Catholic religious community, my spiritual home, for all their love, stewardship, and prayers. Cornerstone continues to nurture and incarnate the Old Catholic eucharistic character of the local Church in its liturgy, which speaks more eloquently than the words contained in these pages. Thank you for feeding my spiritual life as a priest and baptized member of the body of Christ.

I owe gratitude and joy to my life partner, John P. Webster, for tolerating the several years of preoccupation with the research and writing of this book. Without his patience, wisdom and dedicated love my book would have never seen the light of day! His faithful support helped ease the sometimes arduous moments in the passage of completing this work.

Lastly, I give glory and gratitude to our triune God who shows me everyday what it means to live the eucharistic life of blessedness in communion with Christ, my fellow sisters and brothers, and all of creation.

Preface

THE HISTORICAL ORIGIN AND THEOLOGY of the Old Catholic Church is largely unknown, misunderstood, and misrepresented in North America. Many self-styled independent Old Catholic authors in the U.S. have successfully adapted the meaning of the term "Old Catholic" to fit their exhaustive ideologies. Essentially these authors have composed a distinctively new understanding of what it means to be Old Catholic apart from and foreign to the Union of Utrecht's eucharistic ecclesiological character. Thus the main thrust of this text ventures to study and examine the complex veritable historical origins of the Old Catholic Church as well as its eucharistic ecclesiology of the local-universal church. Moreover, it will present an authentically contemporary understanding of Old Catholicism as a unified, ecumenical and diverse union of local churches that is truly Catholic, yet independent from Roman Catholic papal authority. Throughout this book I will assert, in one way or another, that Old Catholicism is mostly unknown in North America and deserves greater visibility as well as broader academic attention.

The idea for this book surfaced soon after I began my seminary studies at United Theological Seminary in the fall of 2005. I started to research the subject of Old Catholic history and theology at the seminary library, and soon discovered a wealth of information from various texts and theological journals. This took some "digging" because I had to become creative in my research and think "outside the box" in various ways. Meaning, there was little information on the Old Catholic Church, but a wealth of information about the Jansenist Church, the schismatic churches at Vatican I, Gallicanism, and so on. Through my research I also discovered many inaccurate self-published styled books written by American independent Old Catholic clergy. After reading some of these books I realized that their authors were promoting a theology and history quite foreign to the Old Catholic churches of the Union of Utrecht, in addition to using the term "Old Catholic" in a more broad and novel way. The genesis for this book was also influenced by the Anglican-Old Catholic theologians' conference held at Leeds, England in 2005, which encouraged building better relationships on the local level between the two churches along with seminarian formation in each others' local-universal church. Hence, I have felt compelled to push forward with this work and tersely explicate an accurate and contemporary representation of the Old Catholic Church's complex history and eucharistic ecclesiology in addition to providing a more realistic understanding of the independent Old Catholic churches in North America.

The ultimate purpose of this book is to offer a transformative vision of the nature of the Church as a eucharistic communion, and bring a sense of clarity to the current independent Old Catholic groups in North America. This book is about how Christians theologically view the nature of the Church in the Western world, which always seems to create anxiety among some. This anxiety is heightened especially when it challenges certain perceived normative understandings about God and the Church. In attempting to write such a book like this I do not claim to be an expert of Old Catholic history and theology. The foundational work contained in this text is a product of many years worth of research and academic rigor in a graduate seminary environment. I have earnestly endeavored to be as accurate as possible in representing the history and theology of the Union of Utrecht, as well as clarifying the current independent Old Catholic dilemma in North America. Having prefaced this, I acknowledge that I am first and foremost a student of Old Catholic eucharistic ecclesiology and I invite productive feedback from you, the reader, concerning the content presented in these pages.

Introduction

by Fr. Bjorn Marcussen, Old Catholic Theologian

TO MY KNOWLEDGE THERE HAS NOT been a somewhat comprehensive presentation of Old Catholic ecclesiology published in English apart from the proceedings of the joined Anglican-Old Catholics Theologians' Conference in Leeds, 2005, published as a special edition of the Old Catholic theological journal, *Internationale Kirchliche Zeitschrift* in 2006.

Father Robert W. Caruso's book is a well researched and passionately argued presentation in English of the Old Catholic understanding of the dynamic nature of what the Nicene Creed describes as the "one, holy, catholic and apostolic Church." Father Caruso has researched and found sources in English from a rare collection—from an English translation from 1874 by Hyacinthe Loyson on "Catholic Reform," through translations into English of St. Irenaeus of Lyons and St. Gregory of Nyssa via nineteenth, twentieth, and twenty-first century publications, including variously published articles by Old Catholic theologians Sigisbert Kraft, P.J. Maan, Peter-Ben Smit, and Jan Visser.

There are many small and often inaccurate introductions to the history of the Old Catholic Church. In Chapter One of his book, Father Caruso does an excellent job of untangling the history of the different Old Catholic churches, especially the synodal principle that animates the Old Catholic understanding of the Church's nature.

In Chapter Two, Father Caruso describes comprehensively how Old Catholic ecclesiology sees the Church—local and universal—as grounded in the inner life of the Holy Trinity: dynamic and with unity in diversity, and as an organic community rather than a legal and legalistic entity. The development of the Old Catholic Trinitarian ecclesiology towards an ecclesiology of Communion owes much to Greek Orthodox theologian John D. Zizioulas. Father Caruso does not mention, but I believe it to be an important observation, that the Old Catholic Department of Theology at the University of Bern, Switzerland, for a number of years had a teaching position that always was filled by an Orthodox theologian. Numerous Orthodox theologians did their doctoral research and were awarded their degrees at the Old Catholic Faculty of Theology in Bern.

Of special interest for North Americans is Chapter Three, titled "The North American 'Old Catholic' Predicament." It is, at times, brutally honest and painful to read, a call to those North Americans, mostly clergy who claim to possess Old Catholic orders, to examine their claims and even their existence in the light of Old

Catholic ecclesiology and wider theology. Father Caruso compares the Old Catholic Trinitarian and communion ecclesiology embodied in the synodal principle with the North American redefinition, chiefly by former Congregational minister Karl Pruter as a universal movement. North American self-defined Old Catholics, mostly persons in holy orders, thus deny the fundamental Old Catholic ecclesiological principle of the local church as the embodiment of the fullness of the whole or universal church, and create another entity above or parallel to the local church in which persons receive apostolic succession (narrowly defined as 'valid' orders) to be exercised entirely without reference to the local church as that entity that discerns, calls, elects, and in communion with other local churches, ordains its bishops. North American Old Catholicism seems to mirror a society of consumers of religion and sacramental rites rather than the place where, through the celebration of the Eucharist, the body of Christ unites in communion and community. Independent North American Old Catholic bishops and priests perceive themselves as entrepreneurs. Father Caruso challenges that perception on theological grounds and rejects it as not authentic to the Old Catholic ecclesiology and theology of orders.

Finally Father Caruso makes a bold plead for the possibility of living an Old Catholic identity within the already existing local church in North America: The Episcopal Church. Such an attempt was made when René Vilatte was ordained priest by the Old Catholic bishop of Switzerland for the Episcopal Diocese of Fond du Lac in 1885, and it proved a disaster. The vision sketched by Father Caruso will take theological and personal maturity on both sides to realize.

This book written by Father Caruso is valuable for all who want to know more about authentic Old Catholic theology, the bulk of which is written in German and Dutch and otherwise inaccessible to English-speaking people who do not read either language. Passion and boldness is often absent in academic writings. In this book they work as condiments that create a tasty feast out of something that otherwise is merely bland intellectual fare.

CHAPTER ONE: The Historical Origins of the Old Catholic Church

THE OLD CATHOLIC MOVEMENT[1] is a path that enriches the complex history of the universal church through the ages. The historical complexity of Old Catholicism involves the three different movements that compose the current unified European Old Catholic churches known as the "Union of Utrecht." Each national church belonging to the Union of Utrecht is rooted in its own historical situation and epoch, which testifies to the diversity and independence Old Catholics generally value. This section endeavors to explicate the complex *origins* of Old Catholic history in a concise and fluid manner, so to lucidly illuminate why it merits accurate broader academic attention within the academy of Christian theology.

The Old Catholic churches throughout the world are independent national churches that disagreed with the absolute power of the papacy and the claims of papal infallibility after the Council of Trent (1545-63). This opposition occurred in three separate and distinct historical movements. First, the Old Catholic church of Holland (1724): second, the churches of Germany, Switzerland, Austria, and Czech-Slovakia at the first Vatican Council (1869-70); and lastly, church groups located in North America, Great Britain, Philippines, and the Slavic nations in the twentieth-century leading to the present day. The novelty about these revolutionary movements against the Roman papacy is that they occurred from within the Roman rite (the principal ancient liturgical and canonical) tradition of the Latin rite Western Church.[2] This implies that the genesis of Old Catholicism occurred as a Roman Catholic revolt against papal supremacy in all its forms. It must be clearly understood that Old Catholics never sought to create another church. The difference between Old Catholics and the churches born out of the Reformation is one of local church rights (Old Catholic) verses theological doctrinal differences (Reformation). This stated, Old Catholics still to this day "...do not wish to deny the historical primacy which several Ecumenical Councils and Fathers of the ancient church have attributed to the Bishop of Rome by recognizing him in title as *Primus inter pares* (first among equals)."[3]

The Old Catholic churches are distinctively different from the Protestant, Orthodox and Anglican churches because the genesis of the Old Catholic movement occurred after the late fifteenth to early sixteenth-centuries' Counter-Reformation and Council of Trent (1545-63). These events uniquely established and defined the Roman-rite (i.e., liturgical, canonical, monasticism) of the Catholic church for close to four centuries thereafter (ca., 1563-1869). This stated, Old Catholicism maintained much of its distinctive Roman-rite characteristics in its liturgies and customs (e.g., the centrality of the seven sacraments and the celebration of Eucharist as the summit of the Christian life); and today, Old Catholic communicants, especially those who convert from the Roman church, are content being Old Catholic because of its liturgical similarities with the Roman-rite. It is very much a pietistic affection that is experienced in the heart of every Catholic, which in turn *effects* how one lives his or her life in the eucharistic community of the local-universal church (the Body of Christ).

I. The Conciliar Nature of the Church: A Terse Explanation of its Importance for Old Catholicism

Another distinction of Old Catholicism is its inherent conciliar (non-institutional and dynamic) approach to understanding the nature of the church.[4] In attempting to express their identity that is neither papal nor Protestant/Reformed, the Old Catholic church focused its attention anew having the conciliar nature of the church in mind when theologically explicating questions such as "what is the church?" "How should the church exist in its earthly form?" "How should authority be understood in the church?" The conciliar nature of the church is a complex (and broad) phrase that is difficult to concisely define theologically. It can, however, be described as a concept that moves beyond institutional governance and emphasizes rather the intrinsic relational character of the church between God, human beings and all of creation. This *theanthropic* renewed understanding of the conciliar nature of the church transforms empty theory into an organic constitutive reality of what the Church has always been: an embodied and dynamic catholic (universal) experience of the holy Trinity recognized by faith through freedom and love.[5]

Old Catholic theologians of the Union of Utrecht recognize that conciliarism was a lived experience since the apostolic age of the early church. Since ancient church times, local churches always maintained faith-based relationships with other local churches that would come together in council when important matters needed to be discussed. The conciliar nature of the church was not created but *received* in all humility by humanity as a gift (grace) from God. Further stated, the conciliar church is relational in that it reflects the communal nature of the divine Trinity, celebrating unity in diversity. For this reason the early œcumenical councils, albeit important and foundational to Old Catholic faith and theology, in no way exhaust the conciliar definition of the church. Rather, a council of this sort is an event, a "reflection and manifestation of the conciliar nature of the church."[6]

When the Roman Empire eventually adopted Christianity as its state religion the church gradually moved away from its organic and relational (conciliar) character to a more imperial and sovereign hierarchal power structure, i.e. the centralization of church authority gradually assumed by the pope (the bishop of Rome). It is during the Middle Ages that conciliar ideas resurface amidst the imperial power structure of the papal Western Church through its ecclesiologists and canon lawyers. Conciliar theory eventually evolved into a Western Church historical movement in the mid-thirteenth to early fifteenth-centuries that would rival papal authority, and culminate theory into reality at the great council of Constance in 1414 CE.

The conciliar theory movement in the fourteenth-century was an epic moment in church history because it attempted a major paradigm shift in transferring ultimate ecclesial authority to an ecumenical council, superior even to the pope. The Old Catholic churches of the Union of Utrecht are remnant heirs of the conciliarist movement and cannot be understood apart from it.[7] In order to fully comprehend the complexity of the conciliar movement, a concise study of the internal powers of the early and medieval church's organization is necessary; this implies that medieval canon law, common law, and ecclesiology (theology of the church) are intricately related to the conciliar theory, and conciliarism cannot be fully understood outside these parameters.

Most Catholic canonists and theologians in the medieval church accepted *ipso facto* that the spiritual (*sacerdotium*) powers of the church were superior to that of the temporal (*regnum*) powers of the kingdoms. Further stated, "...for a medieval canonist, there could be no disputing about the 'constitution' of the spiritual hierarchy. The government of the Church was by bishops, and the unity of the Church was ensured by the communion of all its members with a single head, the Papacy."[8] But different theories arose within the bounds of common doctrine among canonists about the "nature of powers implied by papal primacy, on the relationship between the Pope and universal church, and on the internal structure of the Roman church itself."[9] Conciliar theory locates its genesis here in the theories of certain canonistic thought in favor of limiting papal powers of supremacy and jurisdiction in the Roman Catholic Church.

Sophisticated conciliar theories surfaced and were later associated with the Great Schism (1378-1417), when more than one pope claimed authority over the universal Church. Some historians have claimed that the Great Schism created and defined the conciliar theory movement, but other scholars argue that the conciliar theory was not merely an "...accidental or external thrust upon the Church from outside," rather it was more a "...logical culmination of ideas that were embedded in the law and (theological) doctrine of the Church itself."[10] The creation and growth of early medieval church canon law (known as *Corpus Iuris Canonici*) in addition to independent, but very influential, common law interpretations known as the *Decretum*, written by a twelfth-century canonist and ecclesiologist named Gratian of Bologna, helped to evolve and grow the body politic of the Church while exhibiting it as one unified organization subject to its head, the papacy. The medieval canonists were responsible for defining, clarifying and interpreting canon law regarding the powers of the papacy and the rights of the local church. The canonists were diverse in their defining the power of the papacy in this regard, some going so far as to limit the papacy's power under certain circumstances. These treatises left by the twelfth-century canonists would eventually be looked to and utilized by the conciliarists for their most effective arguments supporting their position.[11]

Marsilius of Padua, an early fourteenth-century French scholar, is commonly known as one of the founders of the conciliar movement. He wrote a foundational tome on conciliary theory called *Defensor Pacis* (Defender of the Peace) as a means to combat the unfolding supreme legacy of the pope. His treatise was purely political, and utilized the philosophy of Aristotle and church canon law to argue that "...the basis of all power is the 'the people,' the whole body of believers in the church."[12] William of Ockham was another fourteenth-century conciliar scholar who shared many of the same ideas as that of Marsilius. Some critical scholars today still "hold that the real origin of conciliar thought is to be found in the 'heretical' works of William of Ockham and Marsilius of Padua."[13] Meaning, certain conciliarists knew about the works of Ockham and Padua and quoted them in their own writings, implying that the genesis of conciliarism began with these two men.[14] There is some truth to this observation, however, I concur with Tierney that one must look to the origin of the information used by Ockham and Padua when deciphering the genesis of conciliar thought. In other words, the conciliarists were not so much interested in the peculiar ideas of Ockham and Padua as they were with their citation notes. Further stated,

> ...the Conciliarists preferred to build their systems around doctrines that Ockham (and similarly Padua) himself had borrowed from earlier writers (of the church) and especially from earlier canonistic writers.... The somewhat paradoxical conclusion emerges that Ockham was most influential precisely when he was least original.[15]

Again, I concur with Tierney's main thesis that the ideas of conciliar thought are deeply rooted in the theological doctrines and canons of the church, to which earlier conciliar ideas influenced and impacted the written works of Ockham and Padua.

The above explicated developments on conciliar theory culminated at the ecumenical council of Constance (1414-1418), "...the last council of the Western Church that spoke with one voice."[16] The council was called forth to end the Great Schism of 1378 *and* reform the church.[17] Constance was a unique council because it was evoked by the whole church (lay, clergy, and bishops), and its authority is unquestionably recognized historically in the Roman church to date. The council produced a text entitled *Sacrosancta,* which has been referred to as *the* most revolutionary reform document ever produced by the Catholic Church. The ideas expressed in this ecumenical treatise stated, "The whole Christian community was superior to any prelate, however exalted; the Pope was to be a servant of the Church rather than its master."[18] It is from the council of Constance that a new pope was elected (Martin V), and through this council the newly elected pope (and all his successors) was *canonically* given apostolic authority and succession in the Roman Catholic Church.

This section further argues, based upon the authoritative claims made at the conciliar council of Constance, against the so-called papal divine rights of jurisdictional supremacy over the entire Church and its members, as well as the infallibility of the pope. The council of Constance lucidly proclaimed in its fourth and fifth sessions that "...this holy Synod of Constance, being a General Council lawfully assembled in the name of the Holy Ghost, and representing the Church militant, has received immediately from Jesus Christ a power to which all persons of whatever rank and dignity, not excepting the Pope himself, are bound to submit in those matters which concern the faith, the extirpation of the existing schism, and the reformation of the Church in head and in members," further stated, "...the Council of Constance declared explicitly that a general council is above the Pope, and can judge or even depose him."[19] Clearly, the divine right of the church was *not* to be found in the papacy alone; but rather, it was to be found in the *congragatio fidelium* (the body of the baptized) in general council together as the body of Christ being tenderly guided by the Holy Spirit. Therefore, it can be persuasively argued that the council at Constance, albeit not perfect because it burned John Huss at the stake as a heretic and did not enforce a reform in the church, did *canonically* validate and procure the pope's limited apostolic authority and Petrine succession by the divine guidance of the Holy Spirit. Thus, the current monolithic school of thought in the Roman church—that claims the papacy is *directly* established by the Triune God—was challenged.

Consequently, conciliar theory rather than papal primacy helps to compose the colorful and contextual background needed to fully comprehend and appreciate the Old Catholic movement in lieu of papal supremacy. The council of Constance is significant for Old Catholics because its conciliar authority was real, and it established precedence in the Catholic Church that power can be and should be properly delegated by all the faithful, and not exclusively in the *plenitudo potestasis* (complete power) of the papacy. Hence, the institutional papal claims of divine right of supremacy became the main theological and political crux that would later form the Old Catholic movement in the mid- to late nineteenth-century.

II. The Roman Catholic Church of Utrecht, Holland: A Brief Analysis of its Historical Origins and Significance for the Union of Utrecht

The Catholic Church of Holland is the first and most significant epoch in Old Catholic history because of its ancient origins. This section intends to study the Catholic church of Holland before the schism with the Roman papacy (1724) over the theological issues on grace and local versus universal church authority. Specifically, I want the reader to be acutely aware of how important and influential the local-universal church of Utrecht's history and existence was for the latter nineteenth century Old Catholic churches that formed the Union of Utrecht (1889).

An English man named Willibrord (d. 739) will forever be known as the Catholic bishop who evangelized the area of Europe now known as the Netherlands. He eventually established in the city of Utrecht, Holland his archiepiscopal See (residence)—little did he know how important he would become in the annals of this local church's history. Willibrord was consecrated as Archbishop of Frisia[20] in Rome (695) by Pope Sergious I (d. 701); upon his return to the Netherlands he established residence in the city of Utrecht, which would thereafter always be known as the ancient church see of the Netherlands. Shortly after Willibrord's death Pope Gregory III (d. 741) canonized him a saint and the celebration of his feast day is on November 7.

The see of Utrecht became a temporal as well as a religious authority, controlling a large amount of territory. In the eleventh-century most of Willibrord's successors (the bishops of Utrecht) were "...temporal princes, charged with the duty of defending the frontier of the empire against the Northmen and other invaders."[21] For much of its history, the see of Utrecht would be governed by men of wealthy, noble families. Utrecht's bishops were as actively involved in the geopolitics of Europe as the Roman papacy was prior to the Reformation. Further elaborated, "The bishops, consequently, became warriors rather than prelates; the duties of their pastoral office were frequently exercised by suffragans (assisting bishops), while they themselves headed armies...."[22] To help forge political alliances with these warrior-prince bishops, the popes would grant special perpetual rights to the see of Utrecht in the twelfth-century, which will prove to be important and instrumental to understanding the latter history of Old Catholicism.

The first of these perpetual rights granted to the chapter of Utrecht (members of the cathedral at Utrecht and its surrounding parishes) by Pope Eugene (1145-1153)[23] was the ability to elect episcopal successors to the see in times of vacancy without permission or approval from the pope.[24] The *Fourth Lateran Council* (1215) confirmed this privilege in the council's canons 23 and 24. Another important perpetual right granted to the bishop of Utrecht and the church of Holland by Pope Leo X (1513-1521) in his papal bull *Debitum Pastoralis* was "...the privilege of freedom from the claim of the popes to 'evoke' (prosecute) local causes to be heard at Rome; any attempt to evoke any church case from Utrecht was to be null and void."[25] This bull later proved to be significant when the see defended itself against the Jesuits' indictment of *Jansenism*.

It is true that an austere Augustinian piety helped to form a certain ethos in the church of the Netherlands. A fourteenth-century religious order called the Brothers of the Common Life helped to form this modest piety. Approved by Pope Urban the VI,[26] the order's mission was to fight against ignorance in all its forms through "…teaching the young, sending out preachers, and to recommend the study of Holy Scripture."[27] Its mission was eventually blessed by the bishop of Utrecht and many native Dutch scholars were educated by this order. This austere piety taught by the order and practiced by most in the church of Utrecht preceded *Jansenism* and was uniquely a Dutch expression of Catholicism, which was significantly different from the sentimental cult-like devotions of the Jesuits, i.e. dedication to the sacred heart of Jesus.

The effects of the Reformation nearly decimated the Catholic church of Holland and its episcopal see of Utrecht. Calvinism spread through the Netherlands rapidly in the sixteenth-century. Holland was one of the few countries in the Netherlands that remained steadfast in the Catholic faith despite most of its Protestant Reformed Scandinavian sisters and brothers. Eventually, the church of Utrecht gathered and elected Frederick Schenk as their new bishop. The pope, trying to combat Protestantism wherever he could, consecrated Schenk and gave him the pallium of archbishop; thus elevating the see of Utrecht to an archbishopric. Schenk would become the first Archbishop of Utrecht (1559-1580) since Willibrord.[28]

III. The 17th Century Controversy on Grace and Local Church versus Papal Authority in the Roman Catholic Church

The 17th-century controversy on grace in the Roman Catholic Church occupied some of the greatest minds in France and elsewhere for more than a century and was said to be "the immediate cause of the schism between Rome and Utrecht."[29] This section challenges Moss' assertion, in that it questions whether the controversy of the doctrine of grace was really the *smoke screen* for the deeper issue of forcing a local church to blind obedience toward the perceived universal authority of the papacy and its doctrines. The following paragraphs attempt to clarify this question by laconically studying both sides of the controversy on grace between the Roman Catholic order called the Society of Jesus (or the Jesuits) and the Jansenist party movement, as well as explicate the effects this controversy played on the local church of Utrecht and the latter Old Catholic churches of the Union of Utrecht.

The Reformation in the sixteenth-century divided the western church into Roman Catholic and Protestant. It also created a surge of new and vibrant ideas about ancient church doctrines (teachings) that were considered unreasonable at that time. Protestants and Catholics during this time continued to battle not just each other but also themselves. The Counter-Reformation (now commonly referred to as the Catholic Reformation) in the Roman church is "...the background against which the whole history of modern resistance to the Papacy must be viewed."[30] I concur with Moss' claim that the council of Trent (1545) and its doctrines is a direct product of the teachings of the Catholic-Reformation. The teaching of the infallibility of the pope took root at Trent, and was strongly implied but not made an official doctrine because there was too much controversy among the bishops in defining what it meant. Furthermore the council of Trent truly defined the Roman Catholic rite apart from the other catholic and apostolic traditions (i.e. Eastern Orthodoxy and Anglicanism). The history of modern resistance to the papacy has its origins in the council of Trent and its teachings, as did the Old Catholic movement before and after the first Vatican Council (1869-70).

The Roman church in the seventeenth-century saw a weakening in its temporal power due mostly to the monarchical structure of secular governance being replaced by new national states of government. This new style of democratic governance, independent of papal authority, was clearly becoming popular in France at that time.[31] An effective attack on Protestantism was no longer possible for the Roman church.[32] Therefore, a surge of piety movements in the Roman Catholic Church began to emerge against the opulence of medieval nobility and the secular monarchy in the Catholic-Reformation, particularly in France.

Jesuit influence took root in France causing great controversy for those who embraced the Augustinian teachings of Cornelius Jansen (1585-1638), bishop of Ypres, who was "convinced that the semi-Pelagian Jesuit interpretations of sin and grace must be combated."[33] Jansen's primary literary work was called the *Augustinus*, published two years after his death in Louvain (1640) and reprinted in France that same year. The *Augustinus* was controversial because of its interpretation of Augustine of Hippo's doctrine on grace, which states the sovereignty of God bestows grace as an unmerited gift to fallen humanity (*efficacious grace*). The Jesuits taught something quite different in that they believed humanity's free choice of the will possesses the innate ability to choose whether or not to receive God's gift of grace (*sufficient grace*).

The theory of *sufficient grace* was first promulgated by a Jesuit moral theologian named Luis de Molina (d. 1600) in his book entitled *Harmony of Free Will with the Gifts of Grace* (1588), which emphasized human free will known as *scientia media* ("middle knowledge"); where "according to which God foreknows specific human acts in different hypothetical situations and then confers grace according to foreseen merits."[34] Molina used the teaching of Thomas Aquinas' (d. 1274) understanding that grace comes prior to human will, efficaciously, without choice albeit working within humanity's free will. Molina interpreted Aquinas' theory to mean that God does not give grace outside humanity's willing it, but instead God works within the framework of humanity's free choice of the will creating the novel *middle knowledge* theory for humanity to be able to freely choose the gift being presented by God, while simultaneously maintaining the ultimate goodness of God apart from evil: God sees all the ramifications of cause and effect in the realm of human decisions in its plenitude, and so understands all the possible results based upon those choices the will makes, but God leaves the individual choice of the will to the human person to freely choose the direction of what one wills. Hence, God's free gift of grace works with humanity's free will, and not apart from it. The Jesuits adopted Molina's theory of *sufficient grace* up until the twentieth-century; however even now the "the characteristic of Jesuit theologians has been a notably positive understanding of the relationship between grace and human endeavors (e.g., Pierre Teilhard de Chardin, 1881—1955)."[35]

Jansen, in addition to the Roman Catholic Dominican order, argued that the Jesuits were teaching a semi-Pelagian doctrine, misinterpreting both Thomas Aquinas' theory on grace as well as Augustine of Hippo's (d. ca. 440) teaching on grace and free will. This sixteenth-century controversy predominantly between the Dominicans and the Jesuits was labeled *De Auxiliis* ("concerning the helps" toward salvation). The Dominicans believed they were the true followers of Aquinas' teaching on grace, in which *efficacious grace* from God moves human free will freely. The Jesuits distorted Aquinas' teaching, according to the Dominicans, and had disregarded Augustine of Hippo's doctrine on grace as defined at the Council of Orange (529). Meetings were held between the Dominicans and Jesuits by popes Clement VIII (d. 1605) and Paul V (d. 1621), and the outcome of those meetings was a papal decree (issued in 1607) stating that both sides (Dominican and Jesuit) could teach their differing theologies on grace. Hence, *actual grace* was conceived out of the above controversy, and birthed as official Roman doctrine at the council of Trent (1545-63): the twofold teaching on *actual grace* of the Roman church taught that God's *sanctifying grace* is necessary for one's salvation (this was against Pelagianism), and yet *sanctifying grace* can be resisted (this attacked Jansen's teachings as well as Augustine's doctrine on *efficacious grace*).[36] Clearly the Roman church created its distinctive theological and characteristic expression of Catholicism at Trent.

Jansen's doctrinal ideas in the *Augustinus* were soon

realized in a French convent called Port Royal. The Cistercian convent became the *omphalos* (central location) of Jansen's teachings against the Jesuits. Port Royal was a significant part of French history and was very influential in converting many people, especially France's nobility, to living a strict moral and pietistic Christian life centered on the Eucharist.[37] The so-called *Jansenists* of Port Royal were thoroughly Catholic in that they were loyal to the pope and king of France, but they were labeled as "independent thinkers," which the French monarchy and the pope disliked very much.

King Louis XIV, out of jealousy (because a majority of French nobles were choosing the simple life at Port Royal, and thus rejecting the opulent lifestyle of the French monarchy by these actions), appealed to the pope concerning Port Royal and its popular ascetic movement, which evoked interest by Pope Innocent X, including the Archbishop of Paris and the theological faculty at the University of Paris (the Sorbonne) to study Jansen's book the *Augustinus*. Five propositions of heresy were *extracted* from the *Augustinus* by the University of Paris, which led to Port Royal's demise and the official papal condemnation of Jansen's text as being heretical and put on the Index (by Pope Innocent X's Bull *Cum Ocacasione* of 1653). A controversy immediately ensued about whether or not the five propositions were faithful to Jansen's actual words and ideas—his followers claimed they were not. Soon after these condemnations a *Formulary* was drafted by the French clergy stating that the five propositions of heresy are in the "sense" of Jansen's work in the *Augustinus* (but not necessarily his actual words stated in the propositions themselves), and this said *Formulary* was to be signed by those labeled as "Jansenist" recanting Jansen's work as being a misrepresentation of Augustine's doctrine on grace. The *Formulary* was supported by Pope Alexander VII's Bull *Ad Sacram* (1656).[38]

The Port Royal nuns refused to sign the *Formulary* because they claimed they were not learned enough to understand what they were being asked to sign, but they simultaneously pledged their obedience to the pope and to the Catholic faith on all relevant matters of concern. In 1708 Pope Clement XI suppressed the order and in 1709 the nuns were viciously attacked by France's King Louis XIV because he suspected a political conspiracy behind the independence and wealth of Port Royal. The convent building was decimated by 300 of the king's soldiers, the elderly nuns were exiled into other convents, and the soldiers exhumed the dead bodies of nuns in Port Royal's cemetery and beheaded them as heretics.[39]

Most "Jansenists" in France, fearful of the pope and king, fled to the church of the Netherlands (Holland) for refuge. They were received warmly by the Archbishop of Utrecht (Peter Codde, d. 1710). The five propositions, the *Formulary* (1656), and other decrees of heresy against the "Jansenists" thereafter became instruments for declaring obedience to the pope; the term "Jansenist" became a pejorative label for any person or local church that did not blindly adhere to the pope's will on most, if not all, ecclesial matters.[40] Thus, the church of Utrecht (and Old Catholicism in general), because it did not blindly adhere to papal authority when asked to, was unjustly labeled a "Jansenist" sect.

The term "Jansenist" was extended beyond its original definition of Cornelius Jansen's interpretation of

Augustine of Hippo's theology on grace, free will, and double predestination. Jansen's *correct* interpretation of Augustine's double predestination doctrine was one of the major reasons why the *Sorbonne* (University of Paris) labeled it heretical. The heresy of "Jansenism" was expanded beyond that of Jansen's interpretations of Augustine in the papacy's five propositions, to which it ultimately defined the heresy anew as an instrument against Gallicanism (in France) and conciliarist ideas in general, i.e. promoting education among the laity in understanding scripture, and jurisdictional autonomy to national churches apart from the papacy. *Jansenism* thus became the pejorative (slander) of the day against all parties who questioned or defied the Roman church in any way. It was the militant Jesuit order, dispersed throughout the world as missionaries loyal only to the pope that evolved *Jansenism* into its sectarian meaning perpetuated to date.[41] Interestingly, the Jesuits' role in the sixteenth century is similar to the modern day's phenomenon (for liberal Roman Catholics) of the omnivorous *Opus Dei* (work of God) order in the Roman church: blindly adhering to the pope and Roman doctrine in addition to militantly ensuring that others in the Roman church do the same.

The church of Utrecht was labeled a *Jansenist* church because it protected those individuals who were persecuted and labeled as such (e.g., Pascal). The church of Utrecht counter-argued against the papacy stating that if Jansen, as learned a man as he was about Augustine,[42] was correct in his book about Augustine's teachings (including the doctrine on double predestination), then the church would have to condemn Augustine's teachings as much as it condemned those of his followers. This is but one example of the Roman church's contradicting ideas that Augustine's teachings are acceptable if it comes directly from Augustine, but is heretical if written and taught by a second party.

This leads us back to the question posed earlier in this section as to whether the different teachings on grace between the Jesuits (*sufficient grace*) and the Jansenists in the church of Utrecht (*efficacious grace*) was the *immediate cause* of the schism between Rome and the Catholic church of Holland. Augustine's doctrine on grace was *clarified, defined* and *interpreted* in the Roman church at the council of Orange (529) against the heresy of Pelagianism and semi-Palagianism,[43] but this council did *not decree* Augustine's teaching on grace as *the* official teaching for the catholic (universal) church. It was not until the council of Trent (1545-63) that the official Roman Catholic doctrine on grace and justification was authoritatively decreed by the pope. The promulgation on grace that was born at Trent was the doctrine called *actual grace*, which has already been explicated above. Utrecht and its sister national churches are generally more Augustinian in their theology on grace (adhering more so to the teachings of the ancient council of Orange than that of Trent). However, I disagree with Moss that the *immediate* cause of the eventual split between Rome and Utrecht (1724) was due solely to the controversy on grace between Utrecht and the Jesuits.

The doctrine of grace and free will in the sixteenth-century Roman church (before the council of Trent) was an open theological question for scholars to discern, to which Augustine's teaching (and that of his protégés) was used as a foundational platform to work from. Because there was so much disagreement in the Western Church at that time on the subject of grace (as evidenced in this chapter), it would seem illogical that these theories would be the immediate cause of a schism between Utrecht and Rome; the issue that caused the schism is more complex than a mere disagreement on an ambiguous theological teaching of the church (i.e. grace) that clearly is still theologically not well defined in the Roman church to date. The real issue that caused the immediate schism between these two churches had little to do with the theological doctrine of grace, and had more to do with theological and political issues of power and blind obedience to the papacy above all else.

Jansenism is a term not well defined because of its political and historical affinity with "giving a dog a bad name" to discredit a specific person and/or local church.[44] Theologically, *Jansenism* vaguely refers to Augustine's extreme doctrine of double predestination, which the Old Catholic churches of the Union of Utrecht have always rejected.[45] Complete submission to the Roman papacy, over and above one's own intellect and conscience, has always been deemed a pietistic virtue in the Roman church. Blind submission to the power of the pope was the real issue behind Utrecht's schism with Rome in 1724 as well as the other two movements in the Old Catholic union that proceeded Utrecht in defying papal authority.

Conclusion

This chapter has concisely explicated the complex historical origins of the Old Catholic Church, so to lucidly illuminate why it merits the broader academic attention it has yet to be given within the academy of Christian theology. Further, I believe that church historians have a responsibility (by virtue of their vocational calling) to ensure that the origins of the Old Catholic churches of the Union of Utrecht (as well as its entire history) are taught correctly in all its complexity, so to fully appreciate the diverse and manifold subjectivity of Western Church history in general.

Old Catholic history has been distorted and inaccurately represented for a very long time in North America by many self-published authors. This chapter has endeavored to *responsibly* correct these inaccuracies by explaining the complex *shared* historical origins of the Old Catholic churches of the Union of Utrecht. Old Catholicism's uniqueness lies in its Catholic origins, and its continued commitment to the Cathlic tradition, having severed its ties to Rome, unlike the Protestant and Anglican reformers. That is, the Old Catholic churches of the Union of Utrecht historically purveyed a catholic and apostolic tradition of the ancient church apart from the council of Trent (Roman Catholic), Anglican, and Protestant/Reformed influences. This is not to suggest that the Old Catholic Church outright rejects these other Western Christian traditions, rather Old Catholics merely do not fully embrace the theological stances that these other western traditions have assumed. Further stated, "The Old Catholic view is that mistakes were made on both the Roman and the Protestant sides (with regard to the significance of tradition).[46] The common origins of the Old Catholic Church are centered in the theology of the *ecclesia primitiva* (the early church) having as its foundational base the seven œcumenical councils of the first ten centuries.

The unique historical origins that color the complex history of the Old Catholic Church culminate in a shared ideal of the ancient church and its theology: that the church is one and the fragmented different confessions need to be healed through mutual understanding, humility, freedom, and most of all, love. It is this shared ideal of western historical origins centered in the theology of the ancient church that uniquely positions the Old Catholic Church as a viable means of healing the denominational fragmentation of Catholic, Anglican, and Protestant/ Reformed traditions of the Western Church,[47] while simultaneously bridging the once seemingly unbridgeable gap with the Orthodox churches of the east. Lastly, I end this section with a quotation expressing hope that one day all Christians may appreciate the diverse traditions within the local-universal Churches:

> If Christians approach one another as well as adherents of other religious traditions with respect and humility, then perhaps something new and hopeful will emerge in the future that cannot be anticipated by merely looking to the past.[48]

CHAPTER TWO:
A Trinitarian Image of the Church:
An Old Catholic Perspective

Holy Father, protect them in your name that you have given me, so that they may be one, as we are one.[1]

THE PRAYER THAT JESUS PRAYED for his disciples before suffering the agony of the cross was one of unity. It is a prayer that is both poetic and prophetic because Jesus understood that his disciples would be challenged and hurt on account of the good news. Unity, that oneness of mind and heart in the church that Christ prayed for his disciples would be tested by human egocentricity (individualism), pride, avarice, control and power. Our current reality as Christians is one of dividedness due to these human non-virtues. But as the body of Christ the organic church is compelled to *actively* seek unity as a communion of communities on the local level centered in love, which mirrors the divine relationship of Christ and the Father who are sealed in the love and freedom of the Holy Spirit.

Current Old Catholic ecclesiology affirms that the local-universal church (Greek: **εκκλεσια**) shares similiar characteristics to that of the Holy Trinity. It uniquely participates in the Trinity's divine economy through its filial adoption in Christ constituted in the power of the Holy Spirit. Just as "the Trinity is marked by unity-in-plurality, held together by a bond of love,"[2] so too is the reality of what qualifies *church,* because Christian unity is realized in communion through our common baptism amidst our diversity, and is what (in the end) establishes Christ's mystical body on earth. The church is an *organic community* held together by a bond of love, which is realized through its sacramental (or mysterious) nature, especially through the sacraments of Baptism and Eucharist.[3] The communal and conciliar understanding of the primitive church is uniquely revived in the Western Church through Old Catholic trinitarian and eucharistic ecclesiology.

Old Catholics understand that the essence of what establishes the church as *being church* is through the *local* communion of the baptized (laity, bishop and clergy),[4] which then leads to the affirmation of the idea that Eucharist *is* the manifestation of the Catholic (universal) church on the local level. This chapter aims at explaining the current Old Catholic school of thought on eucharistic ecclesiology. Specifically, each section of this chapter provides a concise historical and/or theological analysis that elucidates the unique whole of mainstream Old Catholic trinitarian and eucharisitic ecclesiology, which has been "…stimulated particularly by Orthodox ecclesiological thought."[5] The Union of Utrecht's contemporary ecclesiological understanding about creation, humanity, God and the church goes beyond institutional convention in what

Greek Orthodox bishop and scholar John D. Zizioulas labels *being as communion*. That is, the ultimate (ontological) nature and purpose of the local-universal church is to *be relational* and not *wholly* institutional. This definitively *organic* and *mystical* conciliar approach toward understanding the nature of the church is what charismatically distinguishes *how* (Greek: *tropos*) Old Catholic ecclesiology is lived out differently from that of Roman Catholic, Anglican,[6] and Protestant/Reform ecclesiology.

I. The Genesis of the Union of Utrecht

The local church of Utrecht, after its schism with the Roman Catholic papacy in 1724, remained in isolation for almost 150 years. It is a church that survived many historical difficulties that often seemed to challenge its very existence. For instance, the strong influence of Reformed Christianity in the Netherlands, most notably Calvinism, threatened to extinguish the Catholic church of Utrecht altogether. However, despite various ecclesial persecutions, the local church of Utrecht maintained its post-Tridentine Catholic identity, both liturgically and with regard to its overall theological understanding of the church. In other words, Utrecht's doctrinal beliefs and liturgical practices remained very similar to that of the Roman Catholic Church's as defined by the Council of Trent in 1545-63. The only perceivable barrier that prevented a reunification between Utrecht and Rome, up and until the mid to late eighteenth-century, was the ongoing disagreement between local church rights versus universal papal supremacy.

Because Utrecht was granted certain papal rights and privileges in the twelfth-century as a Catholic church stemming "from the origin of Christendom in the Low Countries,"[7] Utrecht believed "the Roman Catholic church...caused the breach...by the institution of 'new dioceses' in 1853 [by] erecting opposing altars,"[8] which contradicted prior papal authority and Utrecht's rights of valid apostolic succession received through its first bishop, St. Willibrord. In the end, the Roman church was successful in suppressing Utrecht's identity by simply ignoring its existence (historical and/or otherwise) from the eighteenth-century on; to which this small and seemingly insignificant local church disappeared from the annals of history, only to reappear in the late nineteenth-century weak but strong in spirit amidst the controversy between certain European local church groups and the papal doctrines of universal primacy and infallibility promulgated by Rome at the first Vatican Council of 1869-70.

In the nineteenth-century a resurgence of the conciliar nature of the church was germinating in the local Roman Catholic churches of France, Switzerland, and Germany. Prominent nineteenth-century scholars like German theologian/historian Johann Josef Ignaz von Döllinger (d. 1890) and Austrian philosopher/theologian Anton Günther (d. 1863) were concerned with the increasingly overt legalism and control the Roman papacy was exercising over local national churches. Their extensive scholarly research uncovered numerous misrepresented historical and theological truths being promulgated by the magisterial power of the Vatican in their day. Through the writings of certain ancient church theologians (i.e. the fourth-century works of the Cappadocians as well as other Patristic theologians) scholars like Döllinger and Günther began rediscovering that the nature of the church was not and could not be personified by an *infallible* Magisterium of the Roman Catholic Church or any other outwardly visible human institution *ad se* (in and of itself). Instead, they discovered that "the Church is to be found only where the Spirit is and the apostolic tradition comes to the Church not just through history [human institutions] but as a *charisma* [a gift of God's grace]."[9] Further, ancient understanding of the church's nature is expressed and actualized incarnationally through human gatherings (e.g. ecumenical councils) where ideas are mutually exchanged, and where doctrine is birthed in and for the church through the Spirit-led process of *reception* at the local level. The best, albeit not perfect, expression of this ancient conciliar approach occurred in the ecumenical councils of the first ten-centuries when the church was *ideally* one in the faith.[10] By historically and theologically conceptualizing the nature of the church in this way, theologians like Döllinger and Günther could not but interpret the first Vatican Council as moving "the Latin Church into a new judicial-absolutist legal system and the resulting novel conception of the infallibility of the pope as formulated in 1870."[11] Thus the teachings of Döllinger and Günther, among other similar theologians of their day, were perceived by the Roman hierarchy as a threat to the Roman papacy and its assumed infallible power.[12]

The various late nineteenth-century Roman Catholic theologians mentioned above (i.e. Döllinger) should not be mistakenly misrepresented as being predecessors to the formation of the Old Catholic churches of the Union of Utrecht. Although theologians like Döllinger were very influential to this formation, "it is wrong to describe these theologians as the forerunners of the Old Catholic movement, but they all tend towards the structure and the religious experience of the Early Church as is rejected by the official Church of Rome."[13] Döllinger never wanted to *reform* the church per se. He just could not in conscience uphold the infallibility doctrine of the pope because in his mind there was no historical and/or theological basis within scripture or early church tradition to support such a teaching. He believed that the Roman church was creating a *new* Catholic church, and he wanted no part of it; he would remain an *old* Catholic, faithful to the practices of the early church and its ecumenical councils. Further stated, "Ignaz von Döllinger when addressing Archbishop Scherr of Munich (stated): 'As a Christian, as a theologian, as a historian and as a citizen I cannot accept this new dogma.'"[14] Döllinger's loyalty to the faith and tradition of the Catholic Church was a theme that resounded from many of the baptized in Germany and Switzerland, all the way to Paris, France. Renowned nineteenth-century French Carmelite priest and noted homilist at Notre Dame Cathedral, Fr. Père Hyacinthe Loyson,[15] eloquently expressed a similar piety of the early church stating,

> …I am resolved to abide faithful to the unchangeable faith of the Catholic Church, and the primitive faith of the Church of Rome, I cannot adhere to the new dogma of papal infallibility, in which I see the most dangerous of errors and the most incurable of schisms. "I cannot recognize as truly free and legitimate a Council of which history will say that 'it began with an ambuscade (ambush), and ended with a *coup d'é-tat.'*[16]

The infallibility controversy of Vatican I forced a wide gap between the Roman hierarchy and local church groups (lay and clergy) in countries like Germany and Switzerland in the late nineteenth-century. Furthermore this controversy was *the* preceding event that provoked these sub-ecclesial groups to petition the isolated local-universal church of Utrecht to provide them with bishops so to be able to maintain a eucharistic fellowship (as an emergency local church apart from Rome) until the issue of infallibility could be dealt with properly with the Roman papacy and hierarchy. These groups believed their split with Rome would be short-term, having the idea that some sort of resolution would soon occur between them and the papacy.[17]

The local ecclesial groups in Germany and elsewhere petitioned the local church of Utrecht to consecrate bishops for them partially because they were well aware of Utrecht's history and its unquestionable ancient apostolic succession. Now it is true that the nineteenth-century Old Catholic churches *developed differently* historically from that of the local church of Utrecht, however, when we speak of the theological and historical *origins* between Utrecht and these "emergency bodies of Catholic faithful"[18] one could reasonably conclude that there's not much of a difference between them at all. The similarity between Utrecht and the later Old Catholic churches lies in their characteristically *similiar historical and theological origins*, i.e. emphasizing local church rights over papal authority in addition to teaching and practicing the theological (conciliar) beliefs of the early church, always striving to reunite what was divided in the church. This *similiar relationship of origins* between the local-universal church of Utrecht and the nineteenth-century local-universal Old Catholic churches emphasizes how this ecclesial body can relationally maintain its essentials of the Christian faith as a unified yet diverse church polity to date.

The conciliar events that helped to form the Union of Utrecht in 1889 occurred when Catholic Christians who opposed the Vatican I dogmas met in conference together in Germany (1871) to communicate their hurts, anger, and ideas concerning how they could hold fast to the Catholic faith of the *ecclesia primitiva* (the primitive church).[19] A year after the official closing of Vatican I (1870) and its acceptance of papal primacy (the pope possessing sole authority over all other bishops and the entire church universal) and papal infallibility (the pope's immunity from error in defining matters of faith and morals),[20] Döllinger and twenty-eight other Catholic theologians from all over Europe met in Munich, Germany (September 22-24, 1871) to declare that the Roman church had gone too far and formed a *new* brand of Catholicism by accepting the Vatican dogmas of the infallibility and universal supremacy of the pope; and they further rejected Rome's excommunication letters sent to them as being instruments of power against human reason and modern thought.[21] Those assertions have become historically known as the *Declaration of Dr. Döllinger and his Adherents of 1871*. I am compelled to quote from a section of this *Declaration* as it is presented in Loyson's book, to which I believe strikes at the heart of why these theologians so vehemently rejected and railed against the dogmatic decrees pronounced at the Vatican I Council. Döllinger states,

It is notorious (and if the German bishops do not know it, they ought to) that these doctrines owe their origin to forgery, and their diffusion to violence. These doctrines, as they have been proclaimed by the Pope in the Vatican decrees, strip the fellowship of believers of its essential rights, deny all value to its testimony, destroy the authority of tradition and the fundamental principle of the Catholic faith, according to which Christians are bound to the belief of nothing but what has been taught and believed always, everywhere and by all…. When, now, in their recent pastoral, the German bishops declare that it is Peter who has spoken by the mouth of the Pope, proclaiming himself infallible, it becomes our duty to repudiate such a claim as blasphemy. Peter speaks clearly and intelligibly to us all, in his acts and words reported in the Holy Scriptures, and in his Epistles, which are addressed to us as well as to the primitive Christians. These acts, words, and letters, are animated by a totally different spirit, and contain teachings far other than that which it is now attempted to impose upon us.[22]

According to Fr. Hyacinthe, a series of five conferences were held in Munich (1871) and only two of these meetings have been preserved in writing. One of the two discourses presented was labeled "True and False Catholicism" which reverberated Döllinger's above claims in proclaiming, "We are compelled to make our choice between the faith of the Pope and the faith of the Church…in the words of one of the most learned

Catholics of Germany: 'If the Pope and all the hierarchy become heretical, the Church does not go with the Pope and the bishops. It remains with the faith.'"[23] After this pivotal event it was clear to those who participated in Munich that a separate church polity was inevitably being conceived before their eyes.

The Munich conference was at the median between remaining Roman Catholic and adhering to the Vatican I doctrines, or crossing the line in remaining true not to Rome but to the Catholic Church of the first ten-centuries much like the preceding local church of Utrecht did 150 years ago.[24] Most of the participants at the Munich conference elected to cross the median to try and understand their Catholicism apart from Rome as a separate Catholic communion eventually forming the Declaration of the Union of Utrecht in 1889. The 1889 union declaration of these local European national churches of the Netherlands, Germany, and Switzerland has remained intact since its inception, and its eight articles are what define the polity as a Catholic union of local autonomous churches apart from Rome. The Declaration of the Union of Utrecht is the foundational governing document that "promoted reciprocal integration and the formation of a shared identity among the Old Catholic Churches...furthermore it became clear that only those bishops—*and the churches they represented*—who were admitted to the Union could rightly call themselves 'Old Catholic.'"[25]

The governance and ecclesial structure of the European Old Catholic national churches of the Union of Utrecht are diverse in many ways; however, their ecclesial structures have all been foundationally built upon the synodical/conciliar theory already explained in the previous chapter. Recall that this theory embraces a dynamic style of synodical governance where the laity, on the *local level,* exercises a kind of sovereignty equal to that of the clergy and bishop, each in their own right. Further, this local church (Old Catholic) synodical governance includes and defines the episcopacy from an early church perspective, on which I will elaborate further in section three of this chapter. Suffice it to state here that bishops are the religious leaders of their *local-universal churches*, and have a primary responsibility "...for the local church communion in a different way than is possible according to the universal [imperial] church model of the Roman Catholic coining."[26] The Roman church is oppressively hierarchical in that it has a suppressive top-down ruling structure. Universal governance in the Roman church is centralized in the papacy, not in the *synodos* or gathering of the entire local assembly, and is thoroughly an exclusive way of ruling a church. The conciliary theory of the Union of Utrecht allots much of the governing power to the local churches synods in relation *with* the college of bishops, and embraces an ethos of inclusiveness in encompassing the whole body of Christ in the governance of the local church universal.[27]

A movement called Gallicanism was a type of ecclesial governance that surfaced in France in the fourteenth century that closely resembled the conciliar theory, and was to a certain degree influential in the Old Catholic movement. It has been stated that "the Old Catholic Church movement cannot be understood unless it is recognized as the heir of Gallicanism."[28] In addition to Gallicanism, other politico-national theory movements like Febronianism occurred in the Western Church originating in Germany in the eighteenth-century subordinating ecclesial authority to national interests. Neither one of these movements survived except through the European Old Catholic churches of the Union of Utrecht. It is commonly known among church historians that Gallicanism, and to some extent Febronianism, did not survive because of its "dependence of civil power and academic nature," in addition to lacking "any great spiritual or moral principle."[29] The Old Catholic churches of the Union of Utrecht in the nineteenth-century resurrected some of these local church ideals described above by giving it the needed precedent in a tradition of independence (i.e. Old Catholicism) from the oppressive hierarchal power structure of the Roman Catholic Church.

Interestingly, current Old Catholic ecclesiology embraces Gallicanism and Febronianism to an extent in recognizing that ecclesial governance always begins on the local level in union with other local churches *and* its bishops.[30] It is what Roman Catholic theologian Hans Küng labels a *grass roots* church organizational structure. In lieu of this type of ascendancy one can appreciate the broad freedom in *how* the Old Catholic Church governs itself. Each national Old Catholic church of the Union of Utrecht, i.e. Germany, Switzerland, Holland, Austria, Czecho-Slovakia, Yugo-Slavia, and Poland, is "rooted in its own, specific historical situation."[31] Because of this there are many distinctions between the national Old Catholic churches on the local level from ethnicity and liturgy, to ecclesial constitutions and local governance. Local autonomy is embraced in the Union of Utrecht, however, the national churches "…share one characteristic: they are all founded on the constitutions of the Early

Church as these are laid down in the Ecumenical Councils."[32] The term *unity in diversity* is central to Old Catholic ecclesiology, which derives its theological foundation from two well known early church Fathers: Vincent of Lérins (d. before 450) and Augustine of Hippo (d. 430). Their theological works are important because they convey a broad understanding of catholic ecclesiology from when the church was ideally united as one faith.

When the Old Catholic churches in Europe united together in the nineteenth-century, they sought to unify themselves with each other while remaining true to their way of *being* church. Conformity for the sake of unity was absolutely out of the question, so theologians had to try to find an understanding and articulation for the concept of *unity in diversity*. The Declaration of Utrecht's (1889) first article defines and clarifies the meaning of *unity in diversity* through Vincent of Lérins' best known theological work, the *Commonitorium*, written in the year 434 C.E.; in it we find Lérins' famous, albeit highly generalized, clarification of the Catholic tradition as *quod ubique, quod semper, quod ad omnibus est* (what [has been believed] everywhere, always and by all). This famous statement of Lerins' strikes at the heart of what it means to be an Old Catholic. So long as the *essentials* of the Christian faith are present in the local community—diversity is welcomed, cherished, and embraced.[33] Diversity in its plurality (the many) is genuinely and realistically universal—catholic. The Union of Utrecht's shared contemporary expression of the Catholic Church can be described as "...the communion of the many local Churches. Communion and oneness coincide [naturally]."[34] It is here that Augustine of Hippo's words resonate with Old Catholic ecclesiology in expressing that "Unity [is] in the essentials [of the Christian faith], liberty in the non-essentials, and in all things love [Latin: *caritas*]."[35] The two key words in Augustine's statement are *all* and *love* because Christ commissioned his disciples to preach the good news to *all* of creation (Mark 16:14), and *love* one another as he loved us (John 13:34). Hence, European Old Catholic theologian, Jan Visser, boldly proclaims the,

> ...essential community as the holder of authority, the exercise of which was committed to chosen (lay, ordained, and the episcopate) office holders. The church community is thereby not totally dependent on the authority from above represented by the clergy, but bears the authority in itself. In such a situation the rights of higher authority, such as that of a bishop, return automatically to the lower authorities such as chapters (synodical houses), and so on. They (the Old Catholic Church) preferred an ascending authority to a descending authority.[36]

These above general ecclesiological convictions influence how Old Catholics understand the nature of the church as not just an institution but also, and more importantly, as an organic communal reality that is united in the essentials (amidst difference) to the same Christ who is, who was, and who will for ever be.

Contemporary European Old Catholic theologian Mattijs Ploeger describes the ecclesiology of the Union of Utrecht as gradually developing in three successive historical periods. The first period covers much of what this chapter's section has already elucidated in that the local churches of the nineteenth-century united to try to find a common theological understanding of *being* church. The second period of the Union of Utrecht follows-on into the early twentieth-century where there is a visibly stable, "mainstream Old Catholic theological approach.... It is a period marked by a...self-conscious Old Catholic self-understanding."[37] And the third period known as "mainstream Old Catholic theology" perceptibly tries to maintain a certain measure of continuity among the local churches of the Union of Utrecht from the late twentieth-century to today, having been greatly influenced by Russian and Greek Orthodox trinitarian and eucharistic ecclesiology.

The first period, the inception of the Union of Utrecht, was conceivably the most difficult period because the differences among the local churches trying to unite were comprehensibly more visible than their commonalities. In other words, it took time, energy, and a sense of great humility to come together amidst the differences to try to find a common theological voice as a Union. For instance, the local-universal church of Utrecht held tightly to its "post-council of Trent" Roman Catholic identity and struggled to let go of some of its *Romish* ways of being church. No doubt it took time (decades according to Ploeger) and patience for both Utrecht and the Old Catholic churches born out of the Vatican I controversy to understand and trust each other.

The second and third period of the Old Catholic Church worked from the foundations that were established from the first period described above and formed "specific Old Catholic approaches to catholicity and apostolicity..., whereas for trinitarian and eucharistic concepts of the Church we will have to turn to the third [and most current] period."[38] Because of these seemingly broad historical periods of trying to find a common theological voice in the Union, some have argued that it is quite difficult to find a qualitative theological or spiritual commonality in Old Catholicism because of its visible diversity on the local national level. I assert first, that there is a common qualitatively visible theology and spirituality of the Union of Utrecht; and second, the diversity lies only in *how* each local national church within the Union celebrates the former commonality through its locally diverse customs and traditions. Different approaches to a common theology on the local level is not only acceptable, it is encouraged and celebrated by the Union of Utrecht because, at best, it is trinitarian in concept as we will begin to see more vividly in the next two sections of this chapter. Also, one must realize that "there has always been—and there still is—a school which continues the 'Old Catholic *proprium* [a general commonality]' of the first and second periods, but in a way recognizably influenced by Orthodox ecclesiological thought, particularly its school of 'eucharistic ecclesiology.'[39] My point here is that the local churches of the Union of Utrecht, although independent from each other, are united in a common eucharistic (*koinonia*) ecclesiological character. The categorical *difference* between these local churches, theologically speaking, lies not in *what* is believed, but *how* this common theology is practiced on the local level. Let us now turn to the next section where we will tersely focus on the theological theory of Old Catholic trinitarian Christology, so to better comprehend the *lived* eucharistic and trinitarian nature of the church in the chapters that follow it.

II. Old Catholic Trinitarian Christology

The question Jesus posed to his disciples in the gospel asking "Who do people say that I am,"[40] has continued to engage people throughout history. It still puzzles Christians today because the answers continue to be as diverse as humanity is. Formal teachings about Jesus' life and personhood were culminated and solidified as *dogma* (authoritative teachings of truth) at the œcumenical council of Chalcedon (451 C.E.). The importance of this fifth-century council cannot be underestimated because it provided the local-universal churches with a fairly comprehensive theological and philosophical understanding of Christ's ontological being in relation to God and humanity.

The christological doctrines that emerged from Chalcedon continue to prevail (in the western and most of the eastern churches) as authentic church teachings when discussing the life and personage of Jesus as *Christos* (the anointed one of God). How to implement these teachings in the local body of Christ, so to provide a more *incarnational* (embodied) understanding of why they are significant, is what this section endeavors to study through the eucharistic ecclesiological lens of the Union of Utrecht. Although Old Catholicism is a tradition stemming from the Roman Catholic Church and the Western church in general, it's current theological system of thought, especially in Christology, emphasizes more the Eastern (fourth thru fifth-century) patristic school of thought than that of the Western school, i.e., Augustine of Hippo (d. 430). Further stated, "Contemporary Old Catholic theology has been largely influenced by an [Orthodox] trinitarian approach to the Church...to emphasize variety within unity."[41] This trinitarian approach has undoubtedly influenced how Old Catholic theologians interpret the christological doctrines of Chalcedon.

Most contemporary Old Catholic theologians would concur that Christology is constitutively conditioned by the doctrine of the holy Trinity. Meaning, the council of Chalcedon had to take into account the eternal triunity of the one God in order to logically articulate even its most basic christological premises. Because Greek theological and philosophical ideas permeate the doctrines of Chalcedon, it is essential that we obtain an early church *Greek* philosophical and theological understanding for the term *person* in relation to God and humanity; specifically, we will focus on what it means to assert that Christ shows humanity what true personhood is from an ontological (ultimate being) perspective, in addition to explaining what the divine substance (Greek: *ousia*) of God means in relation to the three persons of the Holy Trinity. Through this terse inquiry, we will come to a clearer theological understanding of *how* the Chalcedonian christological doctrines continue to shape Old Catholic eucharistic and trinitarian ecclesiology as the core *being* of the entire life of the local-universal body of Christ: the church.[42]

Contemplations about the person of Jesus as the Christ emerged almost immediately after his followers claimed he rose from the dead. The early resurrection claims concerning Jesus of Nazareth were "a stumbling block to the Jews and foolishness to Gentiles,"[43] because for the Jew, it was outrageous to claim that God, who is omniscient (all-knowing), omnipotent (unlimited in power), and omnipresent (everywhere), is somehow uniquely present in the humanity of Jesus of Nazareth. The Messiah (anointed one) of Israel was to restore the ancient Davidic kingdom promised by the prophets of the Jewish scriptures, conquer all of Israel's enemies (i.e. the Roman Empire), and bring forth the fullness of God's *Shalom* (blessed wholeness). When considering this Jewish perspective and comparing it with the life and death of Jesus of Nazareth, it seems that at first glance Jesus failed miserably as Israel's anticipated Messiah. Moreover for the Greek philosophical mind, it was unbearable to comprehend, let alone hear, that God's Son was shamefully executed as a criminal on a Roman cross. Amidst all these challenges, it was the ancient "Jesus-believing" communities (that would later assume the title of "Christian" in the late first to early second-century) who were the first to try to explain Christ's unique relationship with the Divine as the Son of God.

While the disciples of the early church were preoccupied with determining Christ's identity in relation to God and the world, they were also simultaneously (and some scholars would add indirectly) outlining the doctrine of the holy Trinity. Paul of Tarsus was not privy to the formal teachings of the Trinity as we are today, but his words in the New Testament epistles (letters) about Christ's relationship (Greek: *schesis*) with the Father and the Holy Spirit undoubtedly alludes to a sort of trinitarian model of God's being. Paul strove in his ministry to elucidate *how* God uniquely relates to the world through the person of Jesus the Christ. The primitive church came to a clearer understanding of God as being Trinity (one God in three persons) through its primary focus on Christ's relationship with God and humanity. The Trinity lies at the heart of the Christian faith. It is only through the doctrine of the

Trinity that Christians can summarize their most profound beliefs about the Father (who is eternally Other)
and the Father's relationship toward humanity and the
world through the very God/very human ontological personage of Christ properly constituted (established) in the
power of the Holy Spirit.

The fourth-century Cappadocian theological pedagogy
of Christ's ontological personhood is of paramount importance when articulating Old Catholic trinitarian
Christology, because it provides an existential (actual existent) meaning to the Chalcedonian doctrines of Christ.[44]
The Cappadocians were revolutionary in their theology
and philosophy because they deviated from the Western
Nicean (neo-Platonic) understanding of God's substance
as possessing "one source extended into three (persons)."[45] Cappadocian theologians like Gregory of
Nazianzus and Gregory of Nyssa redefined the meaning of
the word *person* (Greek: *prosopon*; Latin: *personae*) to mean
hypostasis. This redefining of terms was revolutionary
because the Greek word *hypostasis* was originally synonymous with the word *ousia* (substance).[46] For the
Cappadocians, God's substance is not some naked reality,
but eternally *coincides wholly* in the three divine *hypostases*
(persons) of the one God. Further elaborated, God as
Trinity "is a *primordial* ontological concept and not a
notion which is added to the divine substance or rather
which follows it, as is the case in the dogmatic manuals of
the West...the substance of God, 'God,' has no ontological content, no true being, apart from communion."[47] A
communion centered in the sensuous dance (Greek: *peri-
choresis*) of true love and freedom in the eternal "other."
Personhood and otherness thus become the embodiment

of *how* (Greek: *tropos*) God's divine nature is reflected in the three communal *hypostases* of the Holy Trinity.

It is difficult for humanity to fully comprehend the Cappadocian definition of *person* because "in human existence, nature precedes the person."[48] Meaning, no one human being possesses in his or her person the totality of humanity's nature. This is but a reflection of humanity's fallen condition (a.k.a., original sin) because its nature of communion and ontological personhood (the image of God) was replaced by the exaltation of the *false-self*: the *individual*. Human existence, as an ontological (and relational) commonality of shared personhood, is thus obliterated and distorted when the *false-self* is placed prior to humanity's relational nature. As a result of this fallen condition, humanity's communal nature could no longer exist in love and freedom *with* the particular person because humanity distorted the true notion of personhood by transforming it from an ontological (ultimate) relational particularity of the whole [nature] into a conditional *self* of the whole; thus placing "general being (nature)...ontologically prior to the particular."[49] In this fallen state no one human being can possesses in his or her person the totality of human nature because the particular (person) is now uncontrollably subject to the whole (nature). Thus nature now precedes personhood. As a result of this phenomenon our fallen nature is continuously divided through the act of procreation in that "no human person can be said to be the bearer of the totality of human nature,"[50] and because of this spiraling reproductive force of particularity death occurs so nature can replace particular persons with other particular persons.[51] Humanity, in its fallen state, cannot fathom personhood as internally possessing (through mutual love and freedom) the whole of its nature because the understanding of *person* becomes synonymous with individual: the inward *self* comes before the ontologically relational *other*. No longer can the one and the many exist in communal harmony because the *false-self* precedes all relationships. When humanity turned away from God and focused on the *false-self* for its well being, it was only natural that, as created beings, humanity would deteriorate back into the nothingness from whence it came. This is the "original sin" of humanity. It must be emphasized here that death is made synonymous with sin: they are both non-substantial and antithetical toward being. Hence, death is but the natural result when creatures depend solely on themselves (on their individuality) apart from God's divine gift (grace) of immortality.

The Trinity does not suffer this human fate because God is beyond time and creation, God is eternal. That is, the three *hypostases* (persons) coincide with each other in their one nature apart from space and time, where "multiplicity in God does not involve a division of his nature and energy, as happens with [humanity]."[52] German Reformed systematic theologian Jürgen Moltmann further informs us that the three *hypostases* of the Trinity are equal to each other, and "[b]y virtue of their love they live in one another to such an extent, and dwell in one another to such an extent, that they are one."[53] Each *hypostasis* (person) of the Trinity is in perfect communal unity and equality (Greek: *koinonia*) with the transcendent *other* sharing the one nature and substance of God in eternal love and freedom. Thus the essence of God is communion and relation from all eternity. Greek Orthodox systematic theologian and bishop of Pergamon, John D. Zizioulas, elaborates,

> The mystery of the one God in three persons points to a way of being which precludes individualism and separation (or self-sufficiency and self-existence) as a criterion of multiplicity. The 'one' not only does not precede—logically or otherwise—the 'many', but on the contrary, requires the 'many' from the very start in order to exist.[54]

Some contemporary Western theologians claim that this sort of trinitarian language is more tritheistic than monotheistic because the early church patristic theologians (specifically the Cappadocians) mistakenly begin with the three persons and move from this proposition to describe God's oneness. Most Western theologians struggle with the Cappadocian approach in describing the immanent (intrinsic) Trinity because their theological training stems from such early (western) church teachings as that of Cyprian and most of all Augustine of Hippo.

These fourth and fifth-century theologians, i.e. Augustine, completely transformed trinitarian theology in the Western church by successfully separating the idea of God from the Father

> ...making divine substance a notion (*divinitas*) logically prior to that of the Father, and assigning to it the role of expressing divine unity. The 'one God' becomes thus indentical with the 'one substance', and the problem posed by Arianism [a fourth-century influential movement that stressed Christ was not of the same substance

(*homoousion*) with God the Father, and there was
a time was Christ was not] appeared to be solved
[in the West].[55]

Augustine, assisted in creating a purely Western theological (universal) construct of the Trinity, by attaching
distinctive moral qualities to the persons of the Trinity
when describing their relational unity in the one substance that is God. Fifth-century Greek theologians would
associate these qualities "...as properties common to all
three persons,"[56] and thus disagreed with Augustine,
attaching distinctive psychological and moral qualities to
the different persons of the Trinity in an effort to describe
the one substance of God. The Greek opinion was that
"the only categories we can apply to the persons of the
Trinity are ontological and not moral."[57] What must be
emphasized here is that, according to the Cappadocians as
expressed by Zizioulas and Moltmann, perichoretically
the different hypostatic characteristics of the Trinity that
distinguishes the Father, Son, and Holy Spirit from each
other are exactly what unites them in the eternal fellowship of *agapé*.[58] God's unity does not exist as some naked
substance in itself, but rather exists as personal fellowship—an intense relational life in the other as a Triune
communion.

The Father is the source and unity of the divine substance who eternally begets the Son and from whence the
Spirit eternally proceeds in unending communal freedom
and love. This does not imply that the Father is superior
to the other two persons within the communal triad
because such a notion would eradicate freedom and make
the other two persons subordinate to the Father, making
the Son and the Holy Spirit a *product* of the Father's sub-

stance and not equal to, or *of* the same substance (Greek: *homoousion*). God the Father is almighty (Greek: *pantokrator*) because the substance of God finds its "mode of existence" or source in the eternally related personage of the Father.[59] Moreover, the Father is almighty, not in a subordinating manner, but as having "...the capacity to *embrace and contain*, that is, *to establish a relationship* of communion and love."[60] Each person of the Trinity is thus mutually dependent on the eternal *other* because they subsist together in communal freedom and love with the Father. Zizioulas maintains that the Cappadocians assert "[t]he being of God is identified with the person [of God the Father]."[61] Accordingly then, subordination of the Son and Spirit to the Father does not occur because the communal triune movement happens outside of time, and the Father's *causation* of the other two persons occurs

> ...on the hypostatic or personal level, and not on that of *ousia* [substance], which implies freedom and love: here is no coercion or necessity involved in this kind of causation, as would have been the case had the generation of the Son and the procession of the Spirit taken place at the level of substance.[62]

The essence of the Trinity is the *communio* of the three *hypostases* united together in freedom and love sharing the same nature, while remaining significantly *other*. There is no threat of tritheism (three gods) because God is eternally one in communion and relatedness within God's self. That is, God's essence is not numerical but communal; God is wholly personal and related. It is thus impossible to describe God's essence numerically because only relationship, freedom and love exist apart from the created order. Moreover, difference does not preclude person-hood, but is essential in order to recognize the *other* in the established divine *I-Thou* relationship that is God. Even though there is difference among the divine persons of the immanent (intrinsic) Trinity, their economic (productive) action in creation is done together through their diversity in perfect communal freedom and most of all love (Greek: *agape*). Cappadocian father, Gregory of Nyssa, clearly articulates this immanent and economic relational under-standing of the Trinity and contrasts it to that of humani-ty's plight in stating,

> ...as regards men even if many partake of one activity, each individually set apart work at the thing proposed, sharing in common nothing with the individual activity of those pursuing the same thing.... Therefore, among men, because the activity of each is distinguished, although in the same pursuit, they are properly mentioned in the plural...But in reference to divine nature [of the persons], we have learned that this is not the case, because the Father does something individ-ually, in which the Son does not join, or the Son individually works something without the Spirit; but every activity which pervades from God to creation and is named according to our manifold designs starts off from the Father, proceeds through the Son, and is completed by the Holy Spirit...The action of each [person of the Trinity] in any regard is not divided and peculiar [as it is with humanity's fallen nature].[63]

Thus the unity of the Trinity can be expressed as existing in the tri-unity *hypostatic* relationship of mutual freedom and love that is Father, Son, and Holy Spirit.

This Cappadocian trinitarian pedagogy refers to a truth about humanity, that left to itself, it can never achieve ontological personhood because it loss the "...unique image of the whole"[64] in their relationship with the Triune God thru its misguided dependence on the false-self apart from God. That is why "Christology is founded precisely upon the assertion that only the Trinity can offer to created being a genuine base for personhood and hence salvation [from death: the deterioration back into nothingness form whence it came]." [65] The Chalcedonian definition of Christ as being very human and very divine in his one *hypostasis* (person) implies an understanding of true personhood, because in his person the created (human) being and uncreated (divine) being communally coincide fully, naturally, and undividedly. Christ "...is the revelation of true personhood," to humanity, and thus reflects the fullness of humanity's being made in the *Imago Dei* (Image of God). [66] This *hypostatic union* of Christ's person reflects the immanent communal nature of the Trinity to humanity because in his person the two different natures (very divine and very human) relate in communal otherness to each other in freedom and love. Having stated this, it must be emphasized that Christ *can never* be understood as an individual apart from the communal nature of the Trinity and humanity. Christ's *hypostatic union* unites what was divided by humanity's pride: communion between God, humanity and all of creation established in love and freedom by the Holy Spirit.[67] Christ's very nature is communion and wholeness.

It is important to emphasize the Cappadocian assertion of the Trinity's communal nature when speaking about Christ because he "...does not first exist as one, and then become the many."[68] Christ *is the one who represents the many*; his ontological personhood is the unity that universally relates humanity and creation in all its diversity to the Divine because he does not stand alone, "but rather (eternally and continually) exists in his relationship with (God) the Father,"[69] and is properly constituted (established) in God the Holy Spirit. Christ becomes the *new Adam* because through his incarnation he restores and embodies the full nature of humanity with the full nature of his divinity creating a proper relationship between God and all of creation in his one person. It is through the glory of the incarnation that the *created* and the *uncreated* unite without confusion or division by the power of the Holy Spirit in the one person of Christ, so to have the capacity to conquer death (the consequence of humanity's prideful false-self) and restore the relationship that existed between the divine and the created as in the beginning. The incarnation of the eternal Logos embodies not only the eternal nature of God, but also reunites humanity with the divine (Greek: *theosis*), not through obligation, but in love and freedom.[70] The mystery of the incarnation allows for the possibility of resurrection, which ultimately becomes a reality through the paschal mystery of the cross.

The Western church has historically placed an unhealthy emphasis on Christ's one and only sacrifice on the cross, to which it has transformed the understanding of *sin* from an ontological dilemma into a psychological/moral catagorical phenomenon that stresses a sense of individuality in Christ and humanity. This Western church (*Anselmian*) understanding of Christ's atoning sacrifice on the cross to restore humanity's sinful nature has instilled deleterious human pathologies of shame, fear, and guilt in the psyche of many of the baptized throughout the Western church history. When the cross is overly emphasized, Christ becomes individualized and is "seen objectively and historically [thus a gap is established between humanity and Christ where a vehicle of some sort is needed to bridge this gap].... His spoken words incorporated within the Scriptures and perhaps tradition—transmitted, interpreted, or even expounded through magisterium—all being realized *with the assistance or under the guidance of the Holy Spirit*."[71] Here the understanding of ecclesial truth is associated with Christ's *selfhood* or personal/psychological human identity (e.g. his gender, sexuality, language, and ethnicity to name just a few). This christological school of thought is predominantly represented in Roman Catholic and Protestant/Reformed theology, where the Holy Spirit is merely an ancillary to the baptized in understanding who Christ the individual is. Thus one can see how easy this type of Christology can become *psychologized* to the point where Christ's self becomes the propitiatory sacrifice for humanity to appease an angry God because of its disobedience, and the understanding of sin gets theologically transformed from the ground of nothingness (death) to a matter of moral reordering of one's heart back to God (Augustine of Hippo).[72] Not to mention that the Holy Spirit's role becomes that of an *assistant* to Christ and humanity in accomplishing God's salvific plan. Thus the Holy Spirit *guides the pilgrim church* as it moves through history toward the *eschaton* (end days). This predominantly Western christological understanding described above is flawed because "person" is equated with the self-conscious individual, the intrinsic self; the notion of "personhood" is associated with the isolation of the conscious *self* and is not relationally dependent upon the *other* for its existence. Again, existentially speaking, this mode of reasoning places the self-conscious as constitutively primary to that of personhood and not the *I-Thou* relationship.

Christ's truth is not located in his individuality, but in his ontological personhood. Meaning, Christ is the embodied truth for humanity and all creation because he, as a very *human being* (Son of Man) is our reality for what it means to be wholly and freely relational with each other and with the Divine. God the Holy Spirit does not *aid* us in understanding Christ, but *actualizes* in history Christ as the relational and communal person.[73] The Holy Spirit is not subordinate to Christ, but relates and works *with* Christ in equality and freedom. Christ is truth and communion simultaneously because he is fully God and fully human (*hypostatic union*) in his one person properly established in the Holy Spirit to the glory of God the Father. Further elaborated, this *proper synthesis* of Christ and the Spirit deemphasizes the particular *self* in Christ (i.e. his gender, ethnicity, personality, etc.), and emphasizes rather the trinitarian relatedness between Christ and Spirit. The gospel alludes to this intimate relationship many times, stating Christ was conceived by the Virgin Mary in the power of the Holy Spirit (Luke 1:35); it was the Spirit who anointed Jesus as the Christ (Mark 1:10); and St. Paul tells us that the only possible way one could confess Jesus as the Christ was by the power of the Holy Spirit (1 Cor.

12:3).[74] Zizioulas further clarifies that "...the Father and the Spirit are involved in history, but only the Son *becomes* history."[75] However, Christ and the Spirit together show us the glory of our Triune God as perfect persons related in effecting God's eternal salvific plan for all of creation. Putting it another way, there is always a sense in scripture that Christ and the Spirit work together in equality and love; Christ and the Spirit freely lead, love, and guide each other, so to reveal the glory of God the Father in creation. The Spirit glorifies Christ (John 16:14) and Christ glorifies the Spirit (Luke 24:49) in establishing the *organic church* at Pentecost. And together Christ and the Spirit glorify the source of all that is in complete unity and freedom: the Father. Further stated, "The Spirit is not something that "animates" a Church which already somehow exists. The Spirit makes the Church *be*."[76] We must remember that "to speak of Christ (in the economy of creation) means speaking at the same time of the Father and the Holy Spirit. For the Incarnation...is formed by the work of the Spirit, and is nothing else than the expression and realization of the will of the Father."[77] If we are to understand Christ's person in this way, as a relational entity with humanity and not as an agent of *means* for human salvation, then "...there is no gap to fill by the means of grace" because Christ *is* the means of God's grace for humanity in the Spirit.[78] In the power of the Holy Spirit, Christ's person is universalized and realized as truth and community (1Cor. 12) simultaneously and instantly in the moment of every age: "...the Son (of God) effects salvation (through his life, death and resurrection) by the grace of the Spirit."[79]

It is important to remember here that the doctrines

(teachings) produced at the council of Chalcedon "will remain a 'dogma' devoid of existential meaning unless and until it is translated and lived in an ecclesial way."[80] Christology, properly constituted in the Holy Spirit by the divine will of the Father in the economy of creation, and ecclesiology (theology of the church) are inseparable and cannot be fully understood apart from each other.[81] In other words, the ideas of Christ's person pronounced at Chalcedon as well as the understanding of the Trinity (as it has been concisely explicated here) can only be understood through the life and ministry of the local-universal churches throughout the world: the mystical body of Christ on earth.

The above theological ideas about Christ, the Trinity, and the organic church provides the Old Catholic Church with a theological means to coherently explicate its ecclesial apostolic and catholic existence, while also striving to create true *koinonia* (communion constituted in freedom and love) with the divided Christian church throughout the world. Further stated, "Contemporary Old Catholic theology has been largely influenced by a trinitarian approach to the Church. More fundamentally, this results in an understanding of Christian salvation [through the person of Christ] as the restoration of communion."[82] Humanity is saved in community from its prideful false-self and the emptiness of sin, which is the negation of being and empty minion of death (non-being). Like the thief who was crucified with Jesus we reject the pride of our false-selves and ask, in all humility, "Jesus, re-member me when you come into your kingdom." The Old Catholic churches of the Union of Utrecht are deeply rooted historically and theologically in this restored communal identity, understanding that no baptized person or institution of the church can be primarily elevated or set apart as special from the body of Christ. For instance, the term *primacy* for Old Catholics is simply honorific and not authoritative in any sense of the word because, given its extreme authoritarian manner, primacy *distinguishes, individualizes, and sets-apart* a person or institution from the communion of the whole. It is no wonder, then, that great strides have been theologically taken in the Old Catholic churches of the Union of Utrecht to maintain an ecclesiology of restored communal wholeness (*koinonia*) through the ontological personhood of Christ: the head of the church.

III. Eucharistic Ecclesiology and the Episcopacy: An Old Catholic Perspective

A theological study of the Union of Utrecht's eucharistic ecclesiology emphasizes that Christ is the core of *being* church. Through Jesus' life, death, and resurrection humanity learns about its true communal nature, living and loving God properly in the created order. Put another way, Christ is *the* means of God's grace toward all in creation as "…a unique manifestation in visible form of the authentic [trinitarian] life of God."[83]

Hence, humanity becomes a eucharistic (thank-filled) fellowship "giving thanks with the product of (their) labors upon the gifts of God, and daily rejoicing in fellowship with others in the worshipping society which is grounded in eternity [the local church universal]...that in the Eucharist the 'only authentic conception of the meaning of *all* human life finds its realization.'"[84]

As baptized members of Christ's mystical body on earth we are uniquely related to each other through the Holy Spirit in which the eucharistic seal of Christ as our spiritual food (the *Bread of Life*) nourishes, sustains, and "...dwells in our hearts through faith, as we are being rooted and grounded in love (Eph. 3:17)." It is in the constituting power of the Holy Spirit that Christ's paschal mystery (life, death, and resurrection) becomes an ever-real event for and with the baptized as a eucharistic (thank-filled) community. The Spirit not only makes real this one Christ-event in history, but "*at the same time* (actualizes) Christ's *personal* existence as a body or community."[85] There is no "empty space" between Christ and the Spirit (properly speaking) because through the power of the Spirit, Christ exists as true person and communion of persons both at the same time. In light of this, I intend here to explicate a *reliable* Old Catholic eucharistic ecclesiology from a concise trinitarian and christological analysis, concentrating specifically on the simultaneity of the local-universal church in relation to the identity and role of the ministerial *charismata* (God's gift of grace for ministerial service) of the episcopacy.[86]

Current mainstream theological thought in the Union of Utrecht has intimately connected ecclesiology with a theological understanding of the episcopacy (bishopric). Meaning, Old Catholic ecclesiology and the episcopacy are united together in such a way that it would be very difficult to speak of one without relating it to the other. Nicolas Afanassieff and John D. Zizioulas inform their readers that the early Christians understood the universality of the church differently from how the Western church understands it today. The early Messianic churches understood the term "universal church" to mean "universal churches," plural and diverse. "This means we cannot speak of 'catholicity' and ignore the concrete local Church."[87]

The term "local church" has been the cause of much confusion, especially in the United States because our country is expansive and comprised of particular states that are diverse, yet united together as a nation. When the Old Catholic ecclesiological concept of "local church" is applied to the context of the United States, it is essential to remember the conciliar synodical *ascendancy* of authority practiced by the local churches of the Union of Utrecht. Having stated this, the question that needs further pondering is: what defines "local church?" The International Old Catholic Bishops Conference (the IBC) defines *local church* as "...the assembly of all the faithful *in one place* gathered around the bishop and his presbytery in the celebration of the eucharist."[88] It matters not how large (numerically speaking) the local church is, but merely that it *qualitatively* (or naturally) exists in a given place where the local laity and clergy gather around the local bishop in celebration of Eucharist. A local church that possesses one parish or one hundred parishes can still embody the fullness of the church universal on the local (particular) level.[89] For instance, in a large and diverse country like the U.S. it is unreasonable for a bishop,[90] who does not participate in any visible collegial relationship with other bishops, to claim to have episcopal jurisdiction over a vast geographical region (i.e. the

United States) and correctly define it as a "local church." Granted, I concur that the local church should not *merely* or *solely* be defined by geography, but common sense informs one that "local" relates to a *particular place* among a *particular people* gathered around their bishop in celebration of Eucharist, and is not exorbitantly broad in application.

Contemporary Old Catholic theologians like Sarah Aebersold and Mattijs Ploeger concur with Zizioulas' assertion that the defining elements of *local church* exists when "the bishop is ordained to serve in a *particular place* among a *particular people*."[91] The local church is the *full* embodiment of the universal church because of its qualitative catholic character of communion with other local churches and their bishops. Therefore, it matters not how numerically large a local church is, so long as it exhibits the defining elements of what constitutes *local church* in a particular place. The ecclesiological idea presented here is grounded in the *ecclesia primitiva* (Latin: the primitive church) and in New Testament scripture, specifically with Paul of Tarsus' words in 1 Corinthians 12:12-31, where he acknowledges that the church is one body with many members. Contemporary historical critical methods of the New Testament scripture text further informs us that Paul's epistles were not written to a universal church conglomeration spanning across the globe geographically; Paul was writing to local "Jesus-believing" communities like the one in Corinth informing them that they *are the body of Christ*, saying, "...now you are the body of Christ and individually members of it (1 Cor. 12:27)."[92] Paul clearly informs the ancient community of Corinth that they are the body of Christ, and he further connects the local community at Corinth with other local communities in a sense of *koinonia* (intimate communal unity), which gives rise to a related catholicity among local communities in his epistles.[93]

The Old Catholic Church concurs with current Anglican/Episcopal ecclesiology when it states that the local-universal church is comprised *qualitatively* as a diocese.[94] Consequently, the terms *diocese* and *local church* are interrelated, and represents the particular and universal church simultaneously. What, then, constitutes the local church as universal? Recall the relationship of Christ and the Trinity in the previous section. The local church, as the body of Christ constituted in the power of the Holy Spirit, embodies the full universal nature of the church in its particularity because it is in communion with, and wholly represents the 'other' local churches in its distinctiveness through communal freedom and love centered in Christ. Meaning, the local church mirrors God's triune image wholly and definitely in a specific place as the body of Christ, so long as the local church "lives its catholicity and apostolicity in communion with other local churches. It (universal nature) is *dependent* on this communion."[95] This is similar to the *I-Thou* relationship of the persons of the Trinity: the one cannot exist without the many and the many cannot exist without the one in communal freedom and love. Communion, however, is not conditioned by uniformity among the local-universal churches. In fact, it's the exact opposite of uniformity! The catholicity of the local church is conditioned by its nature as being the *Imago Dei* (image of God)—what it is—and naturally seeks out communion with other churches that possesses this same *essential* nature. Similarity in character does not constitute uniformity in the particular; meaning difference is not something that is rejected, but instead is embraced as being part of its nature because each local church's difference allows it to see all other local churches as significantly 'other' and vice versa, while simultaneously sharing the *same essential catholic nature centered in love and freedom as the body of Christ.*

According to classical Old Catholic theologians like Andreas Rinkel (Archbishop of Utrecht, d. 1979) and Urs Küry (Bishop of Switzerland, d. 1976), the local church's *catholic* or *universal* identity can be defined as "faith or doctrine, organization or ministry, and liturgy or sacraments."[96] This *common* Old Catholic ecclesial identity defined as doctrine, organization, and liturgy is embodied by the local churches of the Union of Utrecht differently in *how* they are lived out (e.g. the local Old Catholic Church of Germany is identifiably different in *how it lives out* its common ecclesial identity from that of Switzerland), but amidst these local differences their *communal* relatedness and missional *common* understanding of catholic identity remains one and the same. The *qualitative image of God* as the body of Christ is seen through its common features, which ultimately elucidates the true salvific nature of the local church universal—to bring the good news of the kingdom of God to all of creation in all its diversity.

The local church is a eucharistic communion of the baptized. Through the sacrament of baptism an individual is received as a relational person into the local body of Christ, sealed with the Holy Spirit, and simultaneously is called by the same Spirit of Christ to celebrate Eucharist as a commemoration of their ecclesial and eschatological

(hope-filled) identity; an identity that is intimately connected to the paschal mystery of Christ's life, death, and
resurrection. The local body of Christ comes together as
often as possible to celebrate their life of thanksgiving in
the culminating liturgical act of Eucharist—to receive,
taste, and participate in the great paschal feast of the fullness of God's Kingdom (Greek: *eschatos*). This idea of
Eucharist moves beyond the elements of bread and wine
as "an objectified means of grace;" to *being* the summation
and central support of the local church's reason for existence because it is Christ's real presence in the power of
the Holy Spirit sustaining, unifying, and empowering.[97]

Through the local-universal church's communion in
Eucharist, Christ breaks down all barriers of fear and dis-
crimination, titles and positions of honor, "manifesting
unity in the midst of difference and to reflect in that way
the being of the triune God."[98] The Eucharist reminds the
local church of their common baptismal identity as *being* a
"thankful people;" and they are compelled by the Spirit to
seek communion in radical hospitality to all other local
churches in the mutual and sensuous dance of *agape* (selfless love) in unity with the triune God. Through the power
of God the Father, Christ in *union with* the Holy Spirit, is
the one who continuously re-members the local-church
universal in the reality of what constitutes Eucharist.
Meaning, the baptized *live out* their (related) ecclesial and
eschatological personhood in the eucharistic mystery of
Christ liturgically, in that they *actively participate* in the
fullness of his paschal mystery that brought God and
humanity at-one-ment with each other. The divine liturgy
of the Eucharist is the apex celebration of thanksgiving
that is also *lived out* in the hum-drum of every day life; it is

the life and summit of what it means to be a baptized member of Christ's body on the local level. This idea of a *lived out* Eucharist as *liturgy beyond the liturgy* is very much an Eastern Orthodox patristic teaching. Romanian Orthodox ecumenical theologian, Ion Bria, in his book *The Liturgy After the Liturgy* expands the idea of what Eucharist is in describing it as a living celebration that continues beyond the sanctuary of the church on Sunday and into the sanctuary of the world on Monday. It is the idea that our baptism is a call to live a unique way of life centered in the life of the Triune God who sustains, nourishes, and strengthens us as God's own mystical body on earth.

The Eucharist, as stated above, is much more than its liturgical event; it is the very *apex* of the entire life of the catholic church! Put another way, "What we are talking about is an interpretation of the Church that is 'eucharistic' and an interpretation of the Eucharist that is 'ecclesial'."[99] Further elaborated, liturgy is *not just* an isolated act of worship on any given Sunday, but is an event of the entire church united together with Christ who dwells in the hearts and minds of the faithful in the power of the Holy Spirit. We are *engrafted* into Christ's personal *hypostatic union* of being, implying that an intimate communion exists between Christ and humanity properly established by the Spirit. Christ's presence is not distant from us, but is always and constantly dwelling in us lovingly by the Holy Spirit (John 14:18-23). The Father's grace (or *gift*) of the Son is *given to us* in the sacrament of Christ's real flesh and blood properly constituted (and given as *gift*) by the workings of the Holy Spirit.[100] Thus, Christ nourishes his church in word and sacrament "because we are members of his body."[101]

The overemphasis of sacrifice and philosophical methods of laboriously trying to explain Christ's presence in the consecrated bread and wine by the Roman Catholic Church in the sixteenth-century against Luther and other Protestant theologians found its genesis in the medieval scholasticism of the Western church (e.g. Thomas Aquinas, d. 1274). This sixteenth-century overemphasis of sacrifice in the celebration of the Eucharist, and carnal teaching of Christ's real presence (body and soul) in the bread and wine became known as the doctrine of transubstantiation solidified at the council of Trent (1545-63). This doctrine became the central subject of debate for most theological treatises on the Eucharist for centuries thereafter in the Western church. Eucharist became transformed into *the Eucharist* in the Western church, being reduced to an objectified liturgical act of "what happens" to the bread and wine after it is consecrated. It is my assertion here that the *philosophical* doctrine of transubstantiation diminishes the profound mystery of Christ's real presence in what constitutes Eucharist to a mere carnal "controlled substance" that places Christ in a box for viewing, and limits the freedom of the Spirit in reducing its power to a mere controlled auxiliary for Christ and the church. Meaning, human reason can and should endeavor to theologically describe in words what is ultimate *musterion* (mystery), but it should not go so far as to suggest *ipso facto* that human reason can concretely describe and define *what* this mystery is in and of itself. The philosophical teaching of transubstantiation elevates human reason to a degree that it should not because it *anthropomortizes* divine *musterion* to the extent that God is no longer mystery to us, but a caged entity concocted by humanity's false idolatrous *self*.

The Old Catholic Church has theologically distanced itself from this limited understanding of Eucharist, and broadens the meaning of Eucharist to its ancient definition as being substantively more than the mere elements received at the Mass.[102] Thus most contemporary Old Catholic theologians teach that the doctrine of transubstantiation is an unnecessary philosophical exercise when discussing the mystery of Eucharist. Old Catholic eucharistic theology redirects and transforms the church's understanding of Eucharist in keeping with the *ecclesia primitiva* (primitive church) understanding that "we (the local church universal) should strive to feel Christ living in us rather than explain the way the communication (of Christ's presence in the elements) happens."[103] The occurrence of Christ's presence in the bread and wine, as his real flesh and blood, is more profound than a *sacerdotal* (sacramental power of a priest) and individualized superstitious notion of an individual priest's recitation of formulary words; it is Christ himself who embodies and defines what the Blessed Sacrament is through his body's gathering to celebrate *leitourgia* (liturgy) in *koinonia* (communal love) with one another, proclaiming the gospel faith (*kerygma*) in thanksgiving to God the Father by serving (*diakonia*) all of creation in Christ's name through the power of the Spirit.[104] Christ's presence in the elements of bread and wine are ultimately *musterion* (mystery) in a most profound, exciting and wonderful way. This defining of Eucharist in no way demeans its significance, but resuscitates and elevates the importance of the Blessed Sacrament in the entire life of the church as it was expressed by the early church (patristic) fathers. Further, this Old Catholic perspective on Eucharist resonates with the patristic fathers' understanding of Christ's personhood as eucharistically embodying the church in a manner which language can never fully and/or adequately express in words.

The body of Christ, the local-universal churches throughout the world, is truly (through faith) the flesh and bone of Christ himself (Eph. 5:30). It is the work of the Holy Spirit that empowered Christ's disciples to have faith in his paschal mystery at the Pentecost event described in the *Acts of the Apostles*, having this same Pentecost event transformed into *events* "...which *are as primary ontologically* as the one Christ event itself."[105] Pentecost established Christ's mystical body on earth in the form of local-universal *events* by uniting the Spirit with the flesh in a manner that allows each human being the freedom to unite his or her spiritual and bodily existence to that of Christ's in the sacrament of baptism. In baptism we are forever synthesized with Christ's communal personhood and, in turn, Christ strengthens us with his body and blood as real food and drink. Hence, the Spirit of Christ unites us to his body and we unite our bodies to Christ in the totality of what Eucharist is, forming his body on earth in the power of the Holy Spirit, working and attesting to God's Word from within us. The Spirit embodies the baptized as members of the living Word of the Father on the local level in communion with all other local churches throughout the world.

Old Catholic eucharistic ecclesiology of the local church universal is incompatible with ideas that single out or elevate individuals or institutions apart from the body of Christ, i.e., *clericalism* (power of the ordained priesthood), *sacerdotalism* (individualized sacramental power of a priest) and *sacramentalism* (the teaching that the sacraments are necessary to salvation). The concept of 'individual' does not exist alone in eucharistic ecclesiology, but *only in communion with* other baptized members of the local church universal. Ministry in the local church (lay and ordained) is not something unique, but belongs to the *communio* (community) that comprises Christ's mystical body on earth by virtue of the Spirit. Hence, "...in a eucharistic ecclesiology, the ministry is understood to be primarily the service of presiding (with) the gathering of the whole people of God in such a way that all (lay and clerical) charisms are enabled to contribute their part to the whole."[106] Ordained ministry is thus *not* understood as an inherent ontological power received by an individual at ordination, but more a recognition of a special charism (gift) given by the Spirit at baptism; to which the charism of ordination is identified and nourished in and by the body of Christ, and finally is realized through the laying on of hands by the local bishop.[107] Because the church *is* the mystical body of Christ, its ministry of apostle, priest, and prophet are first and foremost Christ's ministry. Christ's communal existence is *actualized* by the power of the Holy Spirit through all the diverse ministries of the church! In this kind of christological and pnuematological study of ecclesiology one realizes that nothing is "set-apart" from the local eucharistic fellowship. Hence a "...fundamental implication is that no ministry in the Church can be understood outside the context of the (eucharistic) community."[108] Now that we have established a clearer understanding of Old Catholic eucharistic ecclesiology, let us turn and focus more intently on how this ecclesiology characterizes a more in-depth understanding of the Old Catholic episcopacy.

A. The Eucharistic Communion
between the Local Church and the Episcopacy

The episcopacy in the Old Catholic Church possesses a remarkable spiritual influence for the local church both in role and function. The local bishop holds the full sacramental charism (gift) of what constitutes Eucharist for and with the laity (Greek: *laos*) on the local level. The *charisma* (divinely inspired gift of leadership) of the bishopric, since biblical times, represents the unity of the local church to the wider communion of other local churches. Furthermore, since ancient times, the bishop is considered the head shepherd and teacher of the faith who represents Christ in the totality of what constitutes Eucharist *in communion with* the local church universal. Thus the bishop's charism in the body of Christ is characterized and actualized as *communion* by the Holy Spirit. Administrative responsibility has not been commonly associated with the role of the bishop; however, history does show that bishops in the past were involved in administrative matters of their diocese (the local-universal church), though this is not, and never has been, the bishop's main charismatic gift in the local body of Christ.

The bishop is essential when defining the local-universal church. Meaning, a local-universal church cannot exist without a local bishop, and a local bishop cannot exist without a local gathering (Greek: *synodos*) of the *laos*. Meaning, a local-universal church cannot exist as *catholic* (universal) without a local bishop, and a local bishop cannot exist without a local gathering of the laity. The bishop represents the unity that is Christ amidst the diverse ministries of the church on the local level. That is why, according to Zizioulas, only the bishop has the right to ordain within his local community and *only his local community*. The bishop's purpose "...makes no sense apart from his role as the one through whom all divisions, including those of orders, are transcended...the primary function (of a bishop) is always *to make the catholicity of the Church reveal itself in a certain place*."[109] We must consistently remember throughout this text that the local-universal church is defined as containing the fullness of the church's catholicity in manifesting all the essential components of Christ's mystical body (lay and ordained), in living together as a eucharistic (thank-filled) fellowship—giving all praise and glory to God the Father in Christ, through the Holy Spirit in a particular place around the local bishop. Further stated, "The bishop is the sign of unity in the church. The spiritual centre of this unity is the Eucharist, in which the bishop represents the crucified, risen and real present Christ in the congregation (lay and clergy)."[110]

The core element in describing what the episcopacy is for the Old Catholic Church lies in its structure based on the conciliary theory. The bishop is not a dictator in the church, he is not a "mini-pope." The episcopacy is inherently collegial and represents, above all other things, the simultaneous unity of the local and broader churches as "the communion of people who are saved by Jesus the Christ and reconciled with God and one another."[111] The symbolism of this communion between the local church universal and the bishop is intimately connected with the celebration and essence of Eucharist since biblical times, and as "a particular understanding of the Church, Old Catholic theology (views) the Eucharist as the core of *being* Church."[112] Through the bishop the local-universal church can rightly call itself a eucharistic people because where the people and the bishop are (locally), thereto is eucharistic fellowship and communion with one another. The liturgical celebration of Eucharist is central to the lives of Old Catholics because it is Christ's real and active presence in the bread and wine that is both sacred meal and sacramental sacrifice, which unites Christians together in local community with one another, throughout the world and cosmos.[113] It illuminates why the Old Catholic churches of the Union of Utrecht cannot *just* focus and be known merely on the local level as being catholic (universal); every local church must connect itself to other local churches through the mystery of Eucharist. The collegial ministry of the bishop unites in eucharistic fellowship the local catholic churches in acknowledging that:

> Participating in the salvation by Christ represented in (word and sacrament) every 'church' is catholic in the full sense, but this salvation is not limited to her geographical territory. The community of faith is wider than her borders and belongs to her catholic essence to be connected with other local churches in which she recognizes identical catholic character.[114]

It is through this "communion of local churches" united locally and universally by the charism of the college of bishops that the Old Catholic Church believes in a "covenant of space as well as in essence."[115] Meaning, the fullness of God's salvation in Christ is experienced on the local level through the catholicity and apostolicity of its bishop *together with* all the baptized in the liturgical celebration of Eucharist. Through word and sacrament the local church acknowledges the universality of itself as a communion of communities throughout the world; and commissions the bishop, in covenantal bonds with the local priests and deacons, to "share in a special responsibility and task, caring for the continuation in time of the mission of Jesus Christ and his Apostles."[116] Twentieth-century German theologian Werner Küppers (d. 1980) asserted that the church was nothing more than the lived out celebration of the Eucharist in community with one another and for others. The primary celebrant of Eucharist at liturgy is the local bishop who presides *with and guides* the local church's eucharistic life. Ploeger elaborates,

> Priests and deacons are the representatives of the bishops. In the centre of such a eucharistic ecclesiology is not the 'sacerdotal' priest with his 'power' to consecrate and to absolve—together with an understanding of episcopacy reduced to the 'power' to confirm and ordain—but the bishop as the communal and collegial presider of his laity and clergy. Such an ecclesiology…is exciting, because it re-lives and makes visible the ecclesial reality of the Early Church—the local church of the whole people of God, with its deacons, presbyterium, and bishop united in the common eucharistic celebration.[117]

When referring to the nature of the local bishop's *charismata* (spiritual gifts) Old Catholic theologian Jan Visser states that "the highest ministry in the Church should be the expression of the plurality. The One reflects the Many as can be said of the episcopal office."[118] This statement coincides with the idea that the bishop stands *in persona*

Christi (in the person of Christ) *with* the local church universal. Like Christ and all the baptized, a bishop is given the gift of the Spirit to carry out the eucharistic ministries on the local level while simultaneously representing the universality of the local church through the inherent collegial *shared relationship* of ministry with other local bishops. The bishop, however, does not possess or control the Spirit because his ministry is not solely or uniquely his own, just as Christ's personhood moves beyond the individual self in the economy of the Trinity. The eucharistic nature of the church does not allow for the theological idea of inherent or personal "ontological change" in the threefold ranks of ordained ministry in the church. There is no separation between ministry and the body of Christ; there is no one individual that can wholly contain the ministry of Christ and the Holy Spirit. The concept of "setting apart" persons for the ordained ministry is eradicated in the eucharistic nature of the church, and is replaced by Paul of Tarsus' understanding that all ministry flows from Christ in the power of the Spirit and returns back to the Father in all glory, praise, and thanksgiving by the same Christ through his mystical body on earth (Cor. 12:4-31). The local-universal church is the body of Christ whose diverse ministries flow from him in the power of the Spirit, and like a body, the baptized cannot but work together in all its diversity for the glory of the whole. Put another way, it is impossible for the ordained ministry, especially the bishop, to tower over the body of Christ because all ministry is established in Christ's communal personhood and finds its power *through, with, and in* his body by the power of the Spirit; hence, apart from the body there is no authority, there is no validity, there is no ministry!

There is much fear and anger today among some *remnant* (fragmented) Roman Catholics in the United States who feel as though the Roman Catholic hierarchy is slowly and systematically abandoning the progressive spirituality and teachings initiated at the second Vatican Council (1962-65). Generally speaking, there seems to be an ethos of fear and anger between the Roman hierarchy and some American Roman Catholic laity where much needed healing has yet to occur. I believe Old Catholic eucharistic ecclesiology may offer a balm of healing for some of these faithful laity because it is a theology that inclusively relates the episcopacy within the body of Christ rather than exclusively setting it apart from the faithful as a controlling power. This conciliar concept of the episcopacy has been inadequately labeled by some in the past as being nothing less than a "Catholic" version of congregationalism, or a new version of Protestantism.[119] I disagree with this assertion because the bishop's charism still retains a quality of authentic authority in the ecclesial synodical (relational) structure of the local church universal. Conciliarism, as we learned in the previous chapter, goes beyond the political sphere and is at its core a theological concept; it is inaccurate to loosely define conciliarism as merely another word for democracy. At its core, the conciliar church is relational in its *sharing of authority* mirroring the image of the Triune God. Meaning, in the conciliar church, the local bishop is not the sole possessor of *all* authority in the local body of Christ, being that a bishop's authority is not internally or solely realized in the concept of the *self*, but is instead *always in communion with* the local church he serves as well as the college he is part of with other bishops. Consequently, in Old Catholic ecclesiology a bishop is never alone, but is always in *koinonia* (related communion) with the college of bishops *and* the local-universal body of Christ.

B. Church Tradition and the Apostolicity of the Episcopacy: An Old Catholic Perspective

Old Catholic eucharistic ecclesiology affects the very definition and nature of *tradition*.[120] Old Catholics believe that God's channel of revelation comes always through the tradition of the church, where "...it is not obtained, it is received."[121] This semi-Barthian idea of God's sovereignty over revelation (i.e. God and God alone is the one who reveals God's self in creation) is realized in scripture and tradition, but principally through the person of Jesus the Christ as "the *Word*."[122] Although scripture is the primary instrument and channel for tradition, Mann also states that tradition existed through the prophets and apostles before the written word. It is evident here that most Old Catholic theologians view the term *tradition* through the lens of both the authority of scripture and the life of the church throughout the ages; noting that scripture primarily and authoritatively speaks to the lived conciliar tradition of the church. Scripture and the body of Christ coincide and exist together in freedom and love always having its focus on the other; for one cannot exist without the other in an embodied, organic relationship that is centered in *caritas* (love).[123]

The sixteenth-century Protestant Reformation repudiated tradition as a means to revelation, and fell back on the doctrine of *sola scriptura* (scripture alone) because, according to Mann, the post-Trent Roman church started to overemphasize the church institution (German: *Amt*) as being God's revelatory bearer of tradition through its laws, doctrines, and papal decisions.[124] Having this in mind, how do Old Catholics understand the essence and meaning of *tradition* in lieu of the local-universal church and the episcopate? Old Catholic theologians claim that both parties (Roman and Protestant/Reformed traditions) have mistaken one extreme for the other (e.g., scripture over tradition or vice versa). In other words, Old Catholics believe scripture and tradition are inseparable from each other. Scripture and the lived tradition of the body of Christ are particular facets of the one apostolic transmission of the good news. Tradition speaks to the continuity of Christ's mystical body on earth established in the Holy Spirit, through which scripture continually affirms, informs, and supports the church in proclaiming (Greek: *kerygma*) this revealed gospel of what God has done for us in Christ Jesus. In other words, the church is the Bible and the Bible is the church. There is an organic unity that cannot be separated between the bible and the tradition of the church. Further stated, "We (as Old Catholics) believe in the authority of the Church, the living body of the living Christ, which preserves and maintains and transmits to us the Word of its Lord and Head (Christ)."[125] This authority, however, is not purely institutional but *conciliar* in that it is wholly found amidst the entire local body of the baptized (lay, clergy, and bishop) under the guidance of the Holy Spirit (tradition) and Sacred Scripture. St. Paul alludes to this *conciliar* understanding of the church in Corinthians 12, in that as the local body of Christ, the church preserves and maintains and transmits God's Word through its diverse ministries established in the power of the Holy Spirit. Having stated this, let us now turn and reflect on how the conciliar understanding of the church transforms our understanding of the episcopacy as being "…the bearer of tradition"[126] within the local-universal church.

The bishop's sacramental charism represents the communal personhood of Christ as head of the local church, and through this charism he becomes the continuous bearer of the one, holy, catholic, and apostolic tradition. The expression of this continuity is commonly known as "apostolic succession." Old Catholic eucharistic ecclesiology teaches a dynamic understanding of apostolic succession that goes beyond the historical and apostolic "missional" chain of power from bishop to bishop. Recollect that no one person, not even a bishop, can individually possess the diverse gifts of ministry in the local church universal. The continuity of Christ's apostolic ministry is thus rooted in the local-universal church *and* its bishop in a most related and organic way.[127] Historical apostolic succession is an important component to ordained ministry in Old Catholic ecclesiology with regard to the threefold rank in Holy Order of bishop, presbyter, and deacon; however, the bearer of apostolic succession is to be found in the local body of the baptized *in communion with* their bishop who represents Christ in providing and sustaining the ministry of the local church's eucharistic communion. The "succession of the local church" moves toward a different understanding of apostolic continuity. The apostles are no longer seen as historical (individual) figures sent on a mission to spread the good news; instead, the apostles, and thus their successor bishops, are a *college* that represents the *eschatos* (end of history and fullness of God's kingdom) to which Zizioulas further claims that:

> The apostles in their eschatological function are inconceivable as individuals; they form an indivisible college. For this reason they are basically and primarily represented by the college of the Twelve whenever their eschatological function is mentioned (scripturally, e.g. Lk. 22:30). In this case the apostles' relation both to Christ and to the Church is expressed in a way different from that of the historical approach. Here the apostles are not those who follow Christ but who surround Him.[128]

The apostles are Christ's foundation for the kingdom, and the apostolic communities of every age have been built upon this foundation in acknowledging that the kingdom is here in our midst through the local-universal church's communion in the totality of what Eucharist is. Thus apostolic succession "...has to do with the whole church, not just with the ordained ministry." However, it cannot be fully understood apart from the ordained ministry and its continuity with the bishop, because the episcopacy "...expresses the apostolicity of his *Church*."[129]

The constitution of the Old Catholic local-universal church synod in the Netherlands was created in 1921, and later revised in 1973. One of the subject matters addressed in this document was the nature of the episcopacy in relation to the local church universal. After a thorough study on the history of the episcopacy, the following paraphrased idea was created and entered into the revised constitution as a canon stipulating,

> According to the ancient clauses of the *Corpus Luris* (ancient Canon Law of the church of

Utrecht) the bishops still retained all power in spiritual and temporal matters in the church. When composing the new constitution, especially in the revised edition a new course was taken. The accent was no longer solely on the episcopal nature of the church, but also on its synodal nature.[130]

Hence, there is no denying that a bishop has authority in spiritual and secular matters on the local and universal level of the church, but not solely! The nature of the Union of Utrecht's governance requires the college of bishops to be in union with the synodical nature of the local (national) churches. Hierarchal *ex qua non* type of authority does not exist in the Old Catholic Church. The Holy Spirit dwells in all the baptized and, therefore, each baptized person possesses dignity and is given an equal voice in all ecclesial matters. The bishop and the local church (lay and ordained) are united together through its synod in governing the local church universal.

Because the role of the bishop is *apostolic* and spiritually connected to the church as a "eucharistic communion," consecration and election of bishops in the Union of Utrecht is both a local *and* universal event. The local-universal church synod elects its candidate for the episcopacy, and then seeks ratification of its election from its sister local-universal churches through the college of bishops. There must be a spiritual agreement between the local church universal and the college of bishops in the Union of Utrecht when it comes to ratifying and consecrating a bishop. This Spirit-led process of *reception* from the local synod to the college of bishops within the Union is fluid, so long as the local-universal church elected the candidate in accordance with the standards set forth in the *Declaration of Utrecht* (1889) and the *Statutes* of the Union's college of bishops (a.k.a. the *Constitution of the International Bishops Conference*). The college of bishops of the Union of Utrecht are then "asked (by the local communion of the baptized) to consecrate the elected candidate as a bishop (for that specific local church universal), and the consecration takes place after the elected candidate has accepted the obligation, *in connection with* all the other bishops, to maintain the Catholic faith and the responsibility for the progress of the Gospel. In this sense the episcopal ministry is *an eminently ecumenical charge*."[131] The Old Catholic episcopacy is labeled as "eminently an ecumenical charge" because every bishop must respectfully foster the idea of unity in diversity on the local level which simultaneously represents not only the homogeneity of the Union of Utrecht, but also the worldwide (universal) communion of all other local catholic churches together with their bishops (i.e. the Anglican Communion). German Old Catholic theologian and professor at the University of Bonn, Günter Esser, goes further to state that a local bishop is charged to pastor not only his local catholic church, but also other local catholic churches in collegiality (shared authority) with its bishops, emphasizing,

> The IBC (International Old Catholic Bishops Conference) Statute formulates such an *episcope* (oversight) like this: the bishops 'are at the intersection of primary belonging, as individuals (or persons), to their local or national church on the one hand, and of taking, as a college, primary responsibility for the fellowship and communion

of the local and national churches on the other hand.' Collegium means a body of leaders of local churches enjoying equal rights. Standing within a conciliar process, they discuss problems and look for solutions in questions of unity, faith, or discipline which concern the communion.[132]

Clearly, real authority exists in the episcopacy, and it is not monarchical nor is it merely an administrative symbol bound completely to the mercy of the local synod's directives (e.g. a congregationalist-type of governance). The bishop is not a "mini-pope," nor a "pawn" of the local church synod. The bishop's authority is real and is realized in *collegiality* (shared authority and respect) with other local bishops who are in communion with the synodical process of their respective local-universal churches. In accord with Esser, the episcopacy possesses three distinct characteristic dimensions, they are: *personal* in representing the unity of the local church, *collegial* in exercising a shared authority locally and universally in fellowship with other bishops, and *communal* "because a bishop without his (local) flock does not make any sense, as the bishop is rightly to be understood as representing his (local) flock."[133] Through these descriptive "dimensions" the bishop and the local church universal together live out the eucharistic nature of the church in *koinonia* with other local churches and their bishops.

To summarize: The role of the bishop is an important *charisma* in the ministry of the local-universal church, and is symbolically what identifies the local church as apostolic and catholic in all times and in all places. Further, the local eucharistic communion of the baptized in relationship with its bishop, and the bishop's communion (college) with other local bishops, together form the symbiotic relationship that is the local catholic church throughout the world. This is *how* the Old Catholic Church is able to proclaim unity in diversity because the plurality of the body of Christ is centered in Eucharist—Christ's real and sustaining presence represented by the episcopacy both locally and universally at the same time in communion with the body of Christ. Thus the "face" of the episcopacy in the church truly "…should be the person or persons with whom everybody feels at ease, and who is at ease with everybody."[134]

IV. The Celebration of Eucharist: An Active Sign of the Local-Universal Church's Unity in Diversity

The church is the local-universal eucharistic communion of the baptized. Through God's pure gift of love received in baptism, Christians are called to share and celebrate Eucharist and commemorate their identity as an eschatological (hope-filled) people. The liturgical celebration of the Eucharist (the Mass) is where the living body of Christ intimately experiences and receives spiritual sustenance together in holy Communion (the foretaste of the fullness of God's kingdom), expressing and emphasizing the sanctity of the royal priesthood of the baptized on the local level. The local body of Christ comes together as often as possible to liturgically celebrate and fully participate in the eucharistic mystery they are called to live out through their baptism. Together the local church universal unanimously proclaims at the eucharistic liturgy God's great *Amen*—the resounding laud of unity that declares with one voice amidst our diversity: *all glory and honor is yours almighty One, for ever and ever!* This climatic liturgical concurrence acknowledges that Jesus is *Christós* (Christ), the anointed one of God, where the Spirit of unity is located in the gathered assembly's diversity.

This section intends to concisely describe how Old Catholics live out their common eucharistic lifestyle at the local-universal level, both liturgically and theologically. Specifically, we will focus this section's study by briefly commenting on the following questions: what is the sacramentology (study of the sacraments) of the Old Catholic Church? How do Old Catholics celebrate the eucharistic liturgy? What characterizes Old Catholic liturgical worship as being uniquely "Old Catholic?" The answers to the above questions given here are, at best, general in application and I would be the first to acknowledge that a more thorough theological and historical study needs to occur in order to *fully* appreciate the Old Catholic liturgical tradition. This section's aim, however, is to provide *current* and *coherently succinct* answers to the above questions, so to empower the reader in gaining a basic understanding of *how* Old Catholics commonly live out their liturgical eucharistic lifestyle on the local-universal level.

Baptism and Eucharist are the *principal sacraments* in Old Catholic sacramentology.[135] Meaning, the other five traditional sacraments of the church flow from—and locate their power in—the two principle sacraments that Christ himself administered and instituted as evidenced in the New Testament gospel canon. Baptism and Eucharist are constitutively active in the nature of the church itself, and are thus not relegated to being merely one of the seven sacraments as is often the case in the sacramentology of some Western churches. Through the waters of baptism an individual receives God's free gift of divine Grace in the energy (power) of the Holy Spirit. This divine gift given by God to humanity is nothing but the unique participation in God's own communal nature through the Word made flesh: Jesus the Christ. An individual becomes a luminous *person* through the cleansing waters of baptism by dying to evil (corruption and death) and rising to new life as a new creation in Christ; no longer does the *neophyte* (newly baptized person) live for him or herself, but *for* and *with* others in Christ's name as a member of his mystical body on earth: the local-universal church. Baptism intimately links us to Christ's very being (his *hypostasis*), so much so that by the power of the Holy Spirit we become *Christs* to and for the world. Meaning, we become Christ's hands that extend to those in need; his eyes that behold human atrocities; his feet that walk with those going through difficult and joyous times; his lips to kiss and anoint others. In baptism Christ chooses us to be the members of his body and vessels of the Holy Spirit pouring the Father's will into the world.

The sacrament of baptism is a second birth that should be revered as much as our first birth is because it is the new birth of an individual, a person in *communio* with the Triune God and the mystical body of Christ on earth: the local church universal. God gives us new life in Christ through baptism, and nourishes and sustains this new life in the sacrament of Eucharist (Holy Communion). That is why every baptized Christian, no matter what age, is entitled to receive holy Communion for nourishment and strength as a member of Christ's body. Baptism unites us as relational persons to Christ, and thus radically transforms our *being*, creating us anew as partakers of the divine nature of God (2 Peter 1:4). Baptism is *the only sacrament of the church* that ontologically transforms our very being, and forever redirects our lives to live no longer *just* for ourselves but also (and primarily) for God and for our neighbor. As baptized members of Christ's body we become a pneumatological fellowship (*koinonia*) as well as a missional society in proclaiming the gospel to all of creation, preparing for the fullness of God's kingdom on earth by serving others just as Christ came to serve and not to be served (Luke 22: 26-27).

The celebration of holy Eucharist (the Mass) is the apex of the Christian life and *the* climatic celebration of our baptismal communion with the Triune God and all of creation. The local baptized are nourished and strengthened by Christ's body and blood which is real food and drink for the body as well as for the soul. The Spirit constitutes the local-universal church in providing Christ's greatest gift to the baptized: his intimate and active presence in the celebration of the Eucharist throughout the ages. Further, our baptismal unity in diversity is uniquely realized at the Mass where all titles of honor, privilege, and entitlement are eradicated, where the only thing that matters is our communion with each other and with Christ in the fullness of the kingdom where God is all in all. Contemporary theologian, Kathy Rudy, asserts that what unites persons as members of Christ's body is their shared baptismal identity as Christians centered in equality, love, and freedom in articulating:

> What holds Christians together is not wealth or class or human-made law or ethnic background or race or nationality, but rather

> God's self, which is revealed to us through
> our membership (baptism) in the Christian
> Church. Our primary identification is and
> ought to be Christian; any identification that
> takes precedence over our baptism is to be
> avoided.[136]

Thus at the celebration of Eucharist we become known
to each other primarily through our ecclesial identity—
the mark of our baptism in Christ's paschal mystery.

The local church universal comes together in parish
communities to celebrate Eucharist as often as possible,
especially on Sundays, because the totality of what constitutes Eucharist is central to the local churches ancient
catholic and apostolic identity. The baptized, by virtue of
their faith, believe that they are receiving from the altar-
table the real presence of Christ's body and blood in the
consecrated bread and wine. The celebration of Eucharist
memorializes Christ's one and only sacrifice on the cross,
while at the same time actively manifests, in the power of
the Holy Spirit, Christ's one and only *sacrum facere* (the
Latin root word for *sacrifice* which derives its ultimate
source from the early church's Greek conciliatory process
of "making holy") by means of the cross; thus enabling the
whole body of Christ to *sacramentally* perpetuate, actively
participate, and faithfully anticipate the past, present, and
future of Christ's paschal mystery in the celebratory act of
the moment throughout history unto the end of time itself
(the *eschatos*). The celebration of Eucharist further teaches the various parish communities on the local level about
its organic nature centered in fellowship, e.g., being a
family. It sanctifies the intimate human act of dining

together as a household. Christ Jesus provides for us, in the totality of what is Eucharist, a foretaste of the fullness of his paschal feast. Meaning, the local-universal body of Christ is given a glimpse and a taste, in that eucharistic (liturgical) moment, of the kingdom of heaven where *all* are welcome to the paschal table as a diverse household *communio* of God.[137]

The essence of *Church* is much more than a legalistic and bureaucratic instutition, it is a liturgical incarnation of Christ's body formed in the power of the Holy Spirit on the local level. That is, the Christian lifestyle, generated in baptism, views the entire world, and its material elements (e.g., bread and wine), through the eucharistic lens of *sacramentum* (mystery) in, with and through Christ in the power of the Spirit. This public lifestyle of the baptized (Greek: *leitourgia*) is always manifested in *koinonia* on the local level in the power of the Holy Spirit, and attested to in scripture. "The reference is explicit: '...all is yours, and you are Christ's and Christ is God's' (1 Cor. 3:22-23)."[138] The communal celebration of Eucharist on the local-universal level "realizes the authentic nature of the Eucharist"[139] because it activates and sustains Christian unity and its thank-filled lifestyle with the Father through service (*diakonia*), proclamation (*kerygma*), and mission (*leitourgia*). These three interrelated actions are made very real at the eucharistic liturgy, and is afterwards witnessed (*martyria*) in the *liturgical* life and work of the local baptized in the world! This kind of communion is material in as much as it is spiritual, and can only occur when the idealized *I* (the all important modern individual: the *false-self*) is tamed and the heart is redirected *to love outside one's self*, to love both God and neighbor. The body of Christ (the local church) gathers together and celebrates the liturgy of life, the totality of what Eucharist is, always in communion with the other, always in service together for others!

The ancient church rubric of *lex orandi et credendi* (the rule of prayer and belief) is central to understanding what it means to be a living eucharistic (thankful) member of Christ's mystical body in Old Catholic eucharistic ecclesiology. As a gathered priestly assembly on the local-universal level, it is important to reflect on this rubric of prayer and belief by asking ourselves, "how do we pray?" "what do the content of our prayers and liturgical actions mean?" "how does liturgy form our deepest beliefs in (and about) God, humanity, and all of creation?" One way to answer these questions is to focus on the particular *common character* in how Old Catholics celebrate the eucharistic liturgy amidst its more diversely distinctive styles on the local (national) level. Before the *birth* of the Union of Utrecht (1889), there was a surge of liturgical renewal/reformation occurrences happening in Germany and Switzerland as early as 1873 CE.[140] Mind you, this is twenty-six years before the Declaration of the Union of Utrecht was signed into existence. Clearly, one can see the ancient rubric of *lex orandi, lex credendi* at work here in the nineteenth-century liturgical renewal of the Mass in Germany and Switzerland, twenty years prior to the establishment of the Union of Utrecht. The liturgical reform that took place in Germany and Switzerland at that time appealed primarily to the ancient liturgical sources of the early church (e.g., the Hippolytus text), which later influenced the general eucharistic ecclesiological character of the Union of Utrecht in its contemporary liturgical lifestyle as a whole.[141] I find this historical reality fascinating because it essentially *effects* the ancient doctrine of prayer forming belief. Hence, the eucharistic liturgy is the wellspring of life, mission, and identity for the churches of the Union of Utrecht.

Practically speaking, the general *style* of the Old Catholic eucharistic liturgy is uniquely an intimate and warm experience that focuses on the whole community as *the priesthood of the gathered assembly.* This communal character tries to reflect the early churches of the first ten centuries' understanding of the divine liturgy of the Eucharist.[142] German church historian and protégé of Döllinger, Johannes Friedrich, pleaded as early as 1873 that all the baptized (lay and ordained) need to be active participants in the celebration of Eucharist saying:

> For there can be no greater debasement of congregational life than the separation of priest and people that now exists in the Roman Catholic tradition, so that each seems to be praying and acting for himself.[143]

As an *eschatological* (hope-filled) fellowship, Old Catholic communities on the local (diocesan) level continue to gather as often as possible to celebrate their eucharistic lives in an atmosphere of radical hospitality to all who partake in the liturgical celebration of Eucharist. The eucharistic ecclesiological principle of *unity in diversity* is uniquely realized in the Old Catholic liturgy when the local body of Christ comes together as a thank-filled people uniting their personhood and diverse gifts of the Spirit to Christ's personhood, giving glory and praise to God the Creator. The Old Catholic eucharistic liturgy eliminates any semblance of separation (or elevation) of an individual above the rest of the gathered priestly assembly. The altar-table is accessible to all the baptized: the gathered priestly assembly of God's people forming communion together as the local body of Christ in the power of the Holy Spirit. In the Old Catholic Mass God is approachable! In the Old Catholic Mass God is the center of worship and not the ordained priest!

There are liturgical differences on the local level in *how* Eucharist is celebrated, and these local differences are not only acceptable, they are encouraged! Recall that our differences are related to what constitutes our personhood and our communion as the body of Christ. In other words, difference is not only acceptable, it is necessary in order for humanity to participate in the divine personhood of Christ and the transformative power of the Holy Spirit. There is, however, a strong eucharistic ecclesiological character in the Old Catholic Mass both in style and form. At worship the gathered priestly assembly meets together to liturgically celebrate, through Word and Sacrament, *the gift of God for the people of God*: Jesus the Christ. The Old Catholic eucharistic liturgy is divided into two equal and essential parts: the Liturgy of the Word and the Liturgy of the Sacrament. The table of the Word and the table of the Blessed Sacrament are necessary because "both are 'tables' around which the assembly is invited to sit, at which we break open the words of Scripture and break the bread (in forming communion with one another and with Christ in the Spirit)."[144] This *celebrating in community* is what distinguishes contemporary Old Catholic liturgies and gives it its common characteristic. Richard Giles classifies this kind of liturgy of the Eucharist as being "transformative," and indeed it is, because it liturgically activates the holistic reality of eucharistic ecclesiology.[145] Kraft comments further about some of the more particular common liturgical practices of the Union of Utrecht on the local (national) levels stating,

> Nowadays (1960 to present) in the European sees (local-universal churches) of the Union of Utrecht, the celebration of the eucharist with the priest facing the congregation; the regular receiving of communion; the readings and intercessions being done by members of the congregation (who also bring the elements...to the altar)—all this is accepted as quite normal. In small groups the eucharist is celebrated as a table mass, often with a discussion sermon and free prayers. The sign of the cross and genuflection during the eucharistic prayer have gone. In many places the whole congregation joins in the doxology, holds hands during the Lord's prayer and gives one another the peace with great warmth...many congregations also hold weekday services.[146]

The above liturgical characteristics of the Old Catholic Eucharist should be considered as the *essentials* of how Old Catholics characterize their eucharistic worship. These essentials are purposely broad in description and in application, which is yet another liturgical characteristic of eucharistic ecclesiology, so not to impugn diversity and difference in the liturgy on the local level. Liturgical uniformity is not what Old Catholics strive for, but unity amidst diversity, so long as there remains a common *trans-*

formative ethos of essentials in the liturgy that constitutes it as distinctively catholic and eucharistic.

Thus, the Old Catholic churches of the Union of Utrecht are as much a pnuematological gathering as they are a eucharistic fellowship because as local churches they are universally united with Christ in his incarnation, life, death, and resurrection in the Holy Spirit through baptism. The body of Christ on the local level affirms this common baptismal calling of unity in diversity by celebrating Eucharist together in communion with one another, partaking of the one bread, which sustains their ecclesial and eschatological identity given to them by God in the Son, Jesus the Christ (1 Cor. 10:16-17). Old Catholic (eucharistic) worship is dynamic and transformative (in what Giles generally labels as "uncommon worship") because it actively builds community and seeks out ecumenical unity not through laws or doctrines, but through Christ's Spirit of *communion* and *love* in Eucharist, giving all laud and gratitude to the Father of all. Kraft challenges Christian church denominations to rediscover the communal nature of the early church's eucharistic ecclesiology and communal liturgical practices, so to actively pursue ecumenical healing and union where difference is genuinely embraced and a less rigid theological understanding of liturgical essentials are formed in council together. He states:

> If the separated churches of today were to take to themselves the witness of faith and worship which once bound all Christian communities in the East and West, they would be on the path to unity. No one could reasonably say that to do this is not enough, or that it contradicts the basic

statements of the faith and is hence "invalid."
Even the divisive questions concerning the
understanding of the ordained ministry can be
overcome on the basis of the common *lex cele-
brandi* (measure of celebrant's charismatic liturgical authority) and the ancient church's understanding of the *berakah* (thanksgiving prayer
over the gifts)/eucharist and the *epiclesis* (invoca-
tion of the Holy Spirit at the eucharistic liturgy).
For this reason the churches' conversation on
eucharistic fellowship and ministry should move
beyond its present excessive focus on the
accounts of the institution of the eucharist, taken
in isolation.[147]

CHAPTER THREE: The North American "Old Catholic" Predicament

THE OLD CATHOLIC CHURCH is unknown by many in North America.[1] Those who encounter the term "Old Catholic" tend to equate it with either the conservative faction of the Roman Catholic Church or with certain splinter groups known as *Independent Old Catholics*. For most Americans, the Old Catholic Church is a foreign ecclesiastical anomaly. There are, however, some who claim to be affiliated (in some way, shape or form) with the Old Catholic Church. This chapter endeavors to dialogue with and focus on such groups in North America who identify themselves as independent Old Catholics.

First, I feel a need to acknowledge my prior affiliation and participation with one such independent Old Catholic group here in St. Paul, Minnesota (USA). I was ordained to the transitional deaconate and to the ministerial priesthood by an independent Old Catholic bishop who is in the historical apostolic succession of Bishop

Arnold Mathew Harris.[2] I preface this information about myself here because it is important that the reader is aware that the ideas presented in this chapter come from *within* and *not outside* the boundaries of the North American independent Old Catholic phenomena. This chapter intends to illustrate, among other things, the general disorder and erroneous character exuded by the U.S. independent Old Catholics, so to assist them in comprehending their current reality with greater clarity and in greater depth. Secondly, but no less importantly, it must be emphasized that the author's intention here is *not to be baselessly critical or solely polemical* against the U.S. independent Old Catholic jurisdictions who claim (or give the impression) to be associated with the Old Catholic tradition and/or churches of the Union of Utrecht. This chapter strives to remain faithful to my main thesis in *responsibly* articulating the history and theology of the Old Catholic churches of the Union of Utrecht *and* in so doing assist the North American independent Old Catholic jurisdictions obtain a *transformative vision* of a future that offers a more dynamic way of *being* church.

Ultimately, this chapter seeks to accomplish two things: first, to disprove the influentially current, yet misguided American school of thought on Old Catholic history and theology in the U.S.;[3] and second, to clear the build-up of illusory grime that has clogged the minds of so many who associate themselves with this school of thought, so to unclog the transformative and grace-filled pathways that lie ahead for those who want to embrace a more authentic character of the Old Catholic *Way* that is truly universal, missional, and local.

I. The Entropic Character of the "Independent North American Old Catholic Movement"

The current independent Old Catholic, what I deem, *Pruterian* school of thought in North America has successfully contributed to the redefinition of the term "Old Catholic" apart from the Union of Utrecht. This popular school of thought does not *theologically* regard the Union of Utrecht as the defining ecclesiastical body for the Old Catholic faith, and further teaches that the Union of Utrecht is but one manifestation among many within the Old Catholic (universal) movement that is broadly described as "...a number of independent liturgical church bodies who together share two characteristics— they are independent...and they all possess what they claim is a valid apostolic succession in their hierarchal leadership."[4] Thus it is clear that in the U.S. the term "Old Catholic" has been transformed from its perceived "narrow definition"[5] to an all absorbing *universal ecclesiology* that is capable of engaging a multitude of social/moral and disciplinary ideologies exuded by the American independent Old Catholic groups in explicating its way of being church (e.g. acceptance or non-acceptance of certain social moral values, ordination of women, and so on).

The independent Old Catholic groups in North America are scattered and number in the hundreds. To be sure, all one has to do is type the word "Old Catholic" on the Internet and a multitude of American "Old Catholic" Christian communities will surface, each of them claiming independence from the other in a highly individualized and self-determinative manner. There is minimal dialogue and relatedness between the independent Old Catholic bishops in America. That is, collegiality among these bishops (realistically speaking) rarely occurs! The outcome of such exclusive behavior is that each jurisdiction maintains a unique *self* identity that typically mirrors the individual ego of its bishop and clergy, which in the end repels genuine dialogue and authentic relationships (communion) from ever forming amongst themselves. For instance, "communion agreements," or the more popular term of "inter-communion agreements," between two or more small jurisdictions claiming to be Old Catholic occur often in the U.S.; however, these so-called "agreements" are established in a most superficial manner because they are created as easily as they are dissolved. In other words, time and prudence is not allotted for by the independent Old Catholic groups when trying to form fellowship with other like-minded independent ecclesial groups; thus these kinds of hasty actions create a superficial type of relationship that is not worthy of the word *communion*.

Authentic relationships occur between persons, and not solely through individuals or institutions! Jewish philosopher, Martin Buber, points out in his book *I and Thou* that it is only when the *I* can recognize itself, its *being*, in the *thou* (and vice-versa) that genuine relationships occur in real freedom and love.[6] The small self-styled Old Catholic jurisdictions in the U.S. have not achieved this kind of covenantal relationship described by Buber with other independent Catholic jurisdictions. This is so primarily because the focus always seems to be on the individual group's self-preservation; fear and competition are typically the catalysts that cause the independent Old Catholic jurisdictions to connect with each other through so-called "inter-communion" agreements. The focus of these agreements are rarely about forming genuine Christian fellowship (Greek: κοινονια), and more about using the other for its own self-preservation—the idea that if one's church group is in "communion" with another independent church jurisdiction there is less competition and less fear to be had from either side. This competitive behavior that was instrumental in forming such a superficial communion does not dissipate over time, but instead rears its ugly head when any sort of disagreement occurs between jurisdictions. It is, for lack of a better phrase, the *clash of the prideful selves*: the "I am right, and you are wrong" mentality that proves time and again that these so-called communion documents are superficial and reflect a relationship that is not personal (ontologically speaking) but competitive and pride-filled by its very nature. If this were not so, then I believe there would be some qualitative evidence contrary to my above claims. But we are not provided with such an alternative reality of the situation other than the observable truth as stated above, which is set before us within reason.

Karl Pruter's twentieth-century scholastic redefining of Old Catholicism as a *universal movement*, set it apart from the eucharistic eccelsiology of the Union of Utrecht, and aligned it with the more novel concept of *universal ecclesiology*.[7] Having stated this, one can begin to understand why most American Old Catholic clerics typically spend more time teaching and promulgating Old Catholic history rather than its theology. According to most independent Old Catholic theologians, the historical actions taken against the papacy is the precedent of what makes Old Catholics unique and attractive.[8] In other words, the history of Old Catholicism is what makes the movement what it is. Pruter's writings helped to codify (theologically and historically) this novel American understanding of Old Catholicism that exists today.[9]

The *Pruterian* understanding of Old Catholicism in North America theologically embraces a clearly Western (Augustinian) understanding of Trinity, Christology and ecclesiology. Though the bulk of Pruter's pedagogy focuses on church history, a very specific theology emerges from his writings which become part of his overall systematic exposition on Old Catholicism. This convergence of church history and theology is a natural occurrence because the church's history makes no sense apart from attempting to express its theology—apart from its historical relationship with God. Pruter's writings solidified the American school of thought that universalizes the term *Old Catholic* (e.g. as a movement and not as a union of local-universal churches) and transitions the definitive focus of the church (theologically and historically) from the particular to the universal; meaning, the universal whole is emphasized as the source that illuminates itself through particular modes of being (i.e. the local church), which, in turn, accentuates the universal "naked" essence and character of the whole. Pruter thus successfully transformed the term "Old Catholic" into a universal ecclesiology that recognizes every local church as being merely *part of* the whole of the one, holy, catholic and apostolic Church in the world.[10]

The independent Old Catholic ecclesial jurisdictions in North America, that claim to be part of the Old Catholic movement, teach and promulgate much of Pruter's theological and historical ideas. One of the reasons why Pruter's theology has influenced so many independent Old Catholic clerics and bishops through the years is due to an extreme lack of Old Catholic theological scholarship in North America (e.g. Old Catholic theology is taught and written in German for the most part on the local level within the Union of Utrecht). Moreover, Pruter's theological ideas have practically gone unchallenged for at least thirty-five years if not longer! The *Pruterian* school of thought has been the catalyst for creating the different types of American independent Old Catholic groups that currently exist today. It has aided these groups in perpetuating the historical disorder, episcopal fragmentation, and chaotic delusions that a stable and palpable Old Catholic Church in America exists.[11] There are some who still insist that a reliable Old Catholic Church in North America exists, however, this claim is not based on reason but exists rather in the realm of illusion.

Old Catholicism is fairly new to North America, and its history in the U.S. is complex to state the least. Old Catholic history in the U.S. comes to us from two very different sources: 1) the Polish National Catholic Church (USA), which for the most part has a fairly transparent and concrete history; and 2) the independent Old Catholic jurisdictions led by the *episcopi vagantes* (wandering bishops) that stem from diverse lineages of episcopal succession. The history of the latter group is much more erratic and difficult to comprehend than that of the Polish National Catholic Church, mostly because of the sheer number of groups that exist and their lack of solidarity with one another. Our focus will begin with the history of the independent *episcopi vagantes* church groups, and then move to discuss in greater detail the history of the Polish National Catholic Church.

The history of the independent Old Catholic movement

in the U.S. is highly disordered, partially because so many fragmented ecclesial entities have erroneously adopted the term "Old Catholic," e.g., the Old Roman Catholic Church, the Liberal Catholic Church, the churches established by Bishop Vilatte and Bishop Mathew, and so on.[12] This problem developed when more and more self-labled independent Catholic bishops began falsely claiming to be part of the Old Catholic Church. These *wandering bishops* (as they are labeled by Utrecht and the Anglican churches)[13] were, in a manner of speaking, altogether of another ecclesial origin apart from the Old Catholic churches of the Union of Utrecht. The two popular *wandering bishops* that most independent Old Catholic bishops in the U.S. claim for their apostolic succession is Joseph René Vilatte (d. 1929) and/or Arnold Harris Mathew (d. 1919). Let us now reflect briefly on the lives of these two bishops, as well as their influence on independent Old Catholicism in North America.

A. Joseph René Vilatte

Most scholars like Claude B. Moss are reluctant to talk about Bishop Vilatte, and tend to disregard him altogether by asserting that he was not an Old Catholic bishop; but because so many U.S. independent Old Catholic bishops claim to possess Vilatte's historical apostolic succession, we can no longer disregard this history without first providing further clarification on the subject. Further, it cannot be overemphasized that what makes the Vilatte narrative so intriguingly important is not the fact that he was consecrated a bishop in the Jacobite tradition, but that he was first and foremost called, ordained, and sent as an Old Catholic presbyter by the Union of Utrecht to serve an American Old Catholic congregation *within the Episcopal Church (USA)*. Thus Vilatte's importance does not reside in his incessant fixation on becoming a bishop, but rather on his call by an Episcopal bishop to serve a local Old Catholic faith community as a presbyter under his episcopal oversight in America![14] This situation could have been the catalyst for the harmonization of Episcopal and Old Catholic relations in the late nineteenth-century, which could have produced endless possibilities for and with God's people. Unfortunately, this was not to be.

Moss informs us that "the spiritual care of the large number of Roman Catholic emigrants to America, of various nations, who refuse to submit to the Roman Catholic hierarchy in their new country, has long been a serious problem."[15] He goes on to inform the reader that the Old Catholic churches of the Union of Utrecht have unsuccessfully tried to alleviate these contextual conflicts with Rome by establishing Old Catholic mission communities in America. One such occurrence happened in the early nineteenth-century in the state of Wisconsin when, according to Moss,

> At the request of Bishop Hobart Brown, the Anglican [Episcopal] Bishop of Fond du Lac [Wisconsin], Bishop Herzog [the first Old Catholic Bishop in Switzerland, 1876-1924] ordained a young Frenchman, Joseph René Vilatte, on June 7, 1885, to work among French-speaking emigrants in Wisconsin under the direction of the [Episcopal] Bishop of Fond du Lac. The headquarters of the mission (parish) was at a place called Little Sturgeon.[16]

It must be emphasized that Vilatte was ordained a presbyter by the Union of Utrecht only after the Episcopal
bishop of Fond du Lac, Wisconsin requested that the
Union of Utrecht send him a priest to serve a French Old
Catholic community in his diocese. It is not difficult to see
that an emerging relationship between the Anglican
Communion and the Union of Utrecht was beginning to
take root in the late nineteenth-century, even on the most
local of levels. This germinating relationship is made manifest by the gracious overture on the part of the Episcopal
Bishop of Fond du Lac to help a group of French immi-
grant Catholic laity (who did not feel welcome in the
American Roman church nor felt comfortable with the
Episcopal church's style of liturgy) by petitioning for a
presbyter from the Union of Utrecht before an official
communion agreement existed between the two ecclesiastical jurisdictions.

Contemporary American independent Old Catholic
author and bishop in Chicago, André Queen, makes the
claim in his book that there was friction between the new
Episcopal bishop (who eventually succeeded Bishop
Brown in the Fond du Lac Diocese of Wisconsin) and Fr.
Vilatte.[17] Further, Queen gives the impression that Vilatte
came to America on his own accord as an Old Catholic
mission priest, and "...raised and established parishes
with the kindly assistance of the Episcopal Bishop
[Brown] of Fond du Lac."[18] He goes on to state that the
bishops of the Union of Utrecht "...instructed Fr. Vilatte
to separate himself and his parishes from the PECUSA,"[19]
however, Queen fails to support these assertions with
credible source evidence. Hence, one can only conclude
that Queen's historical analysis about Vilatte is not well

researched and contains many inaccurate assumptions. In short, Queen fails to offer credible scholarly support concerning his historical claims made about Vilatte and his priestly ministry in Wisconsin. Not to mention that Queen's book also, in many ways, contradicts Moss' elucidation of the same subject matter.[20]

What is vividly clear is the fact that Vilatte did not like the idea of being a simple parish priest under the authority of an Episcopal bishop.[21] Vilatte wanted to be his own authority and requested that the bishops of the Union of Utrecht provide him with such authority by consecrating him the first Old Catholic bishop for North America. The Old Catholic bishops of Utrecht were reluctant to do this, partially because of their ongoing historical relationship with the Episcopal Church (USA).[22] Eventually, the Union of Utrecht's college of bishops refused to consecrate Vilatte to the episcopacy because they reasoned a local catholic church already existed in the Episcopal Church (USA). Hence, Vilatte's purpose in North America was *not* to establish an Old Catholic Church as a missionary priest, but was instead sent by the Union of Utrecht to serve the Old Catholic community in Wisconsin as an Old Catholic presbyter under the jurisdiction of the local Episcopal Bishop of Fond du Lac, Wisconsin (USA).

The Old Catholic college of bishops further reasoned that if the Union of Utrecht were to establish a bishopric in an already recognized local church universal's geographic location, it would lead to overlapping jurisdiction conflicts that could negatively affect the good relationship occurring between itself and the Episcopal Church (USA). The Union of Utrecht was not willing to jeopardize this relationship to serve "Vilatte's hope of being consecrated

by the Old Catholic Church of Europe...."[23] Clearly there
was no need for an Old Catholic bishop because a local
bishop (in this case an Episcopal bishop) already existed
in an established diocese recognized by the Union of
Utrecht's bishops. Further, the Old Catholic faith tradition
was warmly welcomed and given a place in the Episcopal
diocese of Fond du Lac by its local bishop, and the Union
of Utrecht was not going to disrupt this historical relationship by establishing an opposing bishopric. Thus, one can
only conclude that Vilatte's ambition of becoming a bishop was totally and completely self-serving.

Vilatte was obviously disappointed with the Old
Catholic college of bishops' decision, and soon began
seeking episcopal consecration from any bishop who was
willing to do it. Eventually he was consecrated to the episcopacy by a Jacobite bishop in 1892.[24] Moss elaborates on
Vilatte's new episcopacy by stating, "Vilatte now claimed
to be a Jacobite bishop (though the "Jacobite" Church did
not recognize him or any of his acts), and his connection
with the Old Catholics had ceased...."[25] Vilatte returned
to America and began randomly ordaining priests and
consecrating bishops in the U.S. as well as abroad in different countries, causing much confusion about who he
was and what church he represented.[26] It is unequivocal-
ly clear that independent Old Catholic bishops and clergy
in the U.S. "...who claim to have derived their succession
from [Vilatte] call themselves Old Catholics, but falsely:
Vilatte was consecrated by Jacobite bishops, as we have
seen."[27] Hence, bishops and clergy in the U.S. who derive
their historical succession from Vilatte or other wandering
independent bishops *apart from the apostolic succession of
the Union of Utrecht are not Old Catholic*! Independent bish-

ops of the Vilatte historical succession are of a different ecclesial origin, and to insist that they are Old Catholic[28] is to distort history.

It should also be noted that Vilatte's line of succession has of late been placed under great suspicion because (a) his own consecration was not well documented by credible sources; and (b) even Moss seems to contradict himself in stating that the Jacobite Patriarch *sanctioned* Vilatte's episcopal consecration, and then conversely states that the Jacobite church has never recognized Vilatte nor any of his sacramental actions as a bishop from the beginning.[29] The fact remains that when Vilatte was consecrated a bishop, he was never officially associated with a local church within the historical succession of the apostles. He was very much an independent agent, and this fact sets Vilatte outside *any* communion of the Church.

B. Arnold Harris Mathew

The second most popular historic line of apostolic succession claimed by independent Old Catholic bishops in the U.S. is that of Bishop Arnold Harris Mathew. Unlike Vilatte's dubious episcopal historical succession, Bishop Mathew's episcopacy is unquestionably Old Catholic in origin; he was consecrated to the Old Catholic episcopacy in the late eighteenth-century after being elected by the local Old Catholic church synod of England[30] and presented by its representative to the college of bishops of the Union of Utrecht. Mathew's election and consecration was for the "disenfranchised Roman Catholics" in the local Church of England.[31] Mathew was originally ordained a Roman Catholic priest in Glasgow, Scotland; and he later received a doctorate of divinity from Pope Pius IX.[32]

Undoubtedly, Mathew's theological training and priestly formation was more Roman Catholic than Old Catholic,[33] and this reality, among other things, would eventually become the catalyst of much friction between the Union of Utrecht and himself. The significant difference between Bishop Mathew and Vilatte is the fact that Mathew did not primarily seek the episcopacy for his own benefit. Before his election to the Old Catholic episcopacy, Mathew struggled with his identity as an ex-Roman Catholic priest and vacillated between the Church of England and the Roman Catholic Church.[34] After leaving the Roman Catholic priesthood, Mathew eventually married and sought to fulfill his priestly calling in the Anglican Church. The Church of England, however, was not prepared to immediately accept him as a presbyter without a period of probation (which meant Mathew would not receive a stipendary salary). This probationary period was unacceptable for Mathew because he needed immediate employment to help support his family. So when he was approached in 1908 with the possibility of establishing an Old Catholic mission diocese in England for the disenfranchised Roman Catholics who were not ready to become Anglican, he listened.[35] When considering the circumstances of Mathew's life at this point, it is not difficult to ascertain why he was so willing to serve God's people as an Old Catholic bishop of England.

There were, however, many problems surrounding Mathew's supposed episcopal election in England, and his eventual episcopacy in England was short lived. For instance, the Union of Utrecht did not investigate Mathew's episcopal election thoroughly because if they did they would have realized his election was a hoax—it did not happen. A person named Rev. Richard O'Halloran, a diocesan Roman Catholic priest of Ealing, England,[36] machinated a plan, unknown by Mathew,[37] to establish an Old Catholic mission in England. Mathew became O'Halloran's pawn in achieving his goal: to create an independent Catholic jurisdiction apart from the Church of England. Furthermore the Old Catholic bishops failed to communicate with the Archbishop of Canterbury and the other Anglican bishops "...to find out whether the need for a bishop was genuine."[38] Moss points out that O'Halloran supposedly prevented the bishop of Haarlem (Johannes Jacobus van Thiel 1906-1912) from going to England to conduct such an investigation,[39] but Moss does not cite further evidence in his book to support such a claim. What is clear about this quandary is that the Old Catholic college of bishops failed to thoroughly investigate the circumstances surrounding Mathew's episcopal election. Mathew became the first Old Catholic bishop of the Union of Utrecht who had no local church to gather around him.[40]

Mathew was not isolated though. He still had the support of the Union of Utrecht's college of bishops, and was trying to "...provide a resting-place for disconnected and lapsed Roman Catholics who were not prepared to join the Church of England."[41] Furthermore Mathew tried to create a relationship with the Church of England and "...lectured at the Queen's Hall [in England] in favor of the validity of Anglican orders [which the local catholic church of Utrecht still questioned],[42] and he joined the then new Society of St. Willibrord."[43] The Church of England, however, declared their disapproval of the Union of Utrecht's actions in consecrating a bishop and establishing a rival local catholic church in its ecclesial jurisdiction, "...and on February 22, 1909, the Archbishop of Canterbury wrote privately...pointing out that there was no need for an Old Catholic movement in England, since the Church of England was in the same position as the Old Catholics."[44] After this statement by the Church of England's Archbishop of Canterbury, Mathew's episcopacy became more and more dissonant with the Union of Utrecht as well as the local-universal Church of England. Furthermore, Mathew's actions became more and more unpredictable and detrimental to the Union of Utrecht's college of bishops, and the general relationship between the Old Catholics and the Anglican Communion suffered.[45]

The controversy that alienated Mathew from the Old Catholic college of bishops occurred when he consecrated two Roman Catholic priests to the episcopacy on June 13, 1910 without first consulting his fellow bishops of the Union of Utrecht. Mathew did not follow the *Statutes* that govern the college of bishops' actions. Moreover, Bishop Mathew's conduct was selfish and inappropriate. The Union of Utrecht's college of bishops publicly denounced Mathew's independent consecrations and further stated that he violated the Agreement of Utrecht in four ways: "(a) [Mathew did not inform] his fellow bishops, (b) [the consecrations were conducted] in secret, (c) without assistants, (d) while the candidates were members of another communion."[46] Upon hearing this, Mathew publicly declared his independence from the Union of Utrecht's college of bishops in his now infamous *Declaration of Autonomy and Independence*.[47]

Most of the content contained in Mathew's declaration

are disagreements of discipline and are not doctrinal in nature. Thus, the declaration itself lacks sufficient cause for a schism. Furthermore some of Mathew's claims in the declaration are just incorrect and pernicious toward the churches of the Union of Utrecht. Moss further elaborates that the Union of Utrecht's college of bishops "…regarded [Mathew's] Declaration of Autonomy as an act of separation. The next Old Catholic Conference of Bishops, in 1913, *declared formally that it did not recognize Bishop Mathew or any of his acts.* He had ceased to be an Old Catholic on December 29, 1910, after an episcopate of less than three years."[48] Mathew continued his episcopacy independent of the Union of Utrecht's college of bishops, however, and he continued to publicly claim that he was an Old Catholic bishop.[49]

The actions and teachings of Mathew and Vilatte greatly influenced the history and theology promulgated fifty years later in the writings of Karl Pruter and his contemporaries. The theological and historical ideas that have influenced the independent Old Catholic groups in America today arise from the actions and opinions of Vilatte and Mathew who emphasized independence and individualism over communion and relatedness.[50] Further, the actions and teachings of these two men forever trivialized the theological character of the independent Old Catholic episcopacy, both in how it relates to the local catholic church as well as to other bishops.[51]

Rather than praising the history and actions of these two men—even to the extent of promulgating their theological teachings—the U.S. independent Old Catholic groups should, in all humility, be publicly declaring their regrets for the inappropriate and unfounded schismatic actions both Mathew and Vilatte imposed on Christ's church in North America.

Some independent Old Catholic clergy and bishops in America claim that the Union of Utrecht and the Episcopal Church (USA) have, at least in part, a share in the problems both Vilatte and Mathew encountered.[52] Granted, mistakes were made by both the Episcopal and Old Catholic churches in their dealings with Vilatte and Mathew. However, we must also acknowledge that these were *unique* historical occurrences of "the moment." In other words, the relationship in the early twentieth-century between the Anglican Communion and the Union of Utrecht was very fragile, and so in the cases of both Vilatte and Mathew neither church knew what the outcome would be because it never occurred before. Moreover, the greater politics of the world during this time impacted how churches related to each other, especially how Christians of different denominations viewed the other on the local level. History also illuminates the great patience both the Episcopal and Old Catholic churches showed toward Vilatte and Mathew in trying to work with them. But like the prodigal son in the gospel narrative, the two men were not willing to listen to reason and wanted only from the church what they thought they deserved.

The Anglican Communion and Union of Utrecht acknowledged and learned from the mistakes made with each other in the late nineteenth and early twentieth-centuries, which ultimately strengthened their on-going relationship with one another, allowing them to move forward together in the power of the Spirit.[53] However, it is more than transparent that the U.S. independent Old Catholic groups are paralyzed in moving forward because they exude the independent and individualistic character of their predecessors, Vilatte or Mathew. The Spirit has been suffocated within the independent Old Catholic groups because of this seemingly inherent sense of individualistic pride and intentional isolation from other churches. Hence, I believe a radical paradigmatic transformation needs to occur within the independent Old Catholic groups of America if they truly want to sustain some semblance of a grace-filled life within the greater communion of the church. How to enact such a change is a question that goes beyond our current study, but is an important question nonetheless. No longer can independent Old Catholic groups ignore these divisive realities about themselves, because to do so would be irresponsible to state the least.

The argument that reverberates through most independent Old Catholic groups (promulgated especially by their bishops and clergy) is that Old Catholicism is different in America and should not look to the Union of Utrecht to tell it *how* to be church. I concur with this assertion and so would the Union of Utrecht. What demands further pondering is whether or not the independent Old Catholic churches currently exude and embrace an ethos that could be considered *theologically* Old Catholic in essence? If not, would they be willing to seriously entertain, learn, and reflect with intent on the eucharistic ecclesiology of the church, and actively seek to implement these ideas (practically speaking) on the local level? The reader can decide for her or himself the better answer to these questions. I end this section with a quote taken from the AA *Big Book*, and ask the reader to ponder its wisdom as we move forward in transforming Old

Catholicism in America in and through the power of the Holy Spirit!

> There is a principle which is a bar against all information, which is proof against all arguments and which cannot fail to keep a person in everlasting ignorance—that principle is contempt prior to investigation.   —HERBERT SPENCER

II. The Polish National Catholic Church: The First and Last *Official* Old Catholic Church in North America

The Polish National Catholic Church of America (PNCC) was the largest Old Catholic local-universal church in full communion with the Union of Utrecht. I agree with church historian, Laurence Orzell, when he uses the word *paradox* to best describe the origin and history of the PNCC stating,

> The very fact that the numerically largest Old Catholic churches—the PNCC of America and the Polish Catholic Church of Poland—arose among a people known throughout history for their devotion to the Roman Catholic Church is in itself a paradox. Paradoxical also is the fact that these churches originally emerged not as a result of doctrinal disagreements but rather because of administrative difficulties among Polish Roman Catholic immigrants in the United States at the turn of the century.[54]

A massive influx of Polish immigrants entered the United States from 1880–1914. It was inevitable that the Polish and the Irish (who immigrated to the U.S. in the early nineteenth-century) would encounter conflicts with each other due to different customs and ideas about being church. Sociologically speaking a mutual understanding of each others' diverse social and religious ethnic backgrounds was just not seriously entertained during this time in U.S. history. Social tolerance in the U.S. between the Polish, Irish, and Italians did not occur for some time even though these ethnic groups were of the same Roman Catholic faith and, at times, the same church buildings. There was great social and ethnic conflict in the early twentieth-century between the Polish and the Irish in various larger U.S. cities (i.e. Chicago, New York, Boston, etc.), and the Roman church was not immune to this social problem in the least. Orzell writes,

> The American Roman Catholic hierarchy, composed almost exclusively of bishops of Irish descent, permitted the establishment of Polish parishes but regarded these as a purely temporary phenomenon and favored instead the 'Americanization' of the immigrants. The hierarchy's generally negative attitude towards Polish language and culture clashed with the views of those Poles who nurtured a strong sense of their ethnic identity. The philosophical conflict translated itself into calls on the part of some immigrant laity for a greater role in the administration of parish affairs.[55]

The first well known and well documented Polish-American conflict with the Roman Catholic Church occurred in Chicago, Illinois in 1895, which foundationally helped to create the PNCC.

The conflict was between a Polish Roman Catholic parish and Chicago's Archbishop Patrick Feehan (d. 1902). The Archbishop demanded that the parish hand over its property title and provide the Archdiocese with full control over its property as proscribed by church canon law. The parish as well as its priest (Fr. Kozlowski) eventually decided to severe their relationship with the Roman Catholic Archdiocese of Chicago because no reasonable agreement could be attained between them. The Archdiocese of Chicago was eventually able to strip the parish of its church property, to which the parish responded by building a new church building, and Fr. Kozlowski (who was eventually excommunicated by Archbishop Feehan) blessed it on August 11, 1895. The parish community decided to call their new community All Saints Catholic Church. There was a dilemma, however, in that the new community had no bishop, only a priest. That is, they were a parish living in the Diaspora of the Roman Catholic Archdiocese of Chicago. This was a problem because, in true Catholic fashion, the parish viewed the bishop as being the sign of the church's unity and universality on the local level. The new parish was in a conundrum because it lacked the oversight of a bishop. Thus, the parish could not authentically consider itself part of the local Roman Catholic Church, yet the parish was obstinate in its desire to remain Catholic. This situation gave rise to the ensuing events summarized by Orzell in stating,

> The subsequent spread of the 'Independent' movement and a realization that the profession of Roman Catholicism outside the Roman Church was untenable persuaded Fr. Kozlowski

to establish a formal ecclesiastical alternative for dissident Poles. Elected bishop by his supporters, he approached the Old Catholics [Union of Utrecht college of bishops] for consecration. Following an investigation, the Old Catholics responded positively. Fr. Kozlowski accepted the Declaration of Utrecht and received episcopal ordination in Berne on November 21, 1897 at the hands of Bishop Eduard Herzog, with the assistance as co-consecrators of Archbishop Gerard Gul and Bishop Theodore Weber. Upon his return, Bishop Kozlowski proceeded to consolidate what he called the 'Polish Catholic Church'; he also used the term 'Independent Catholic Diocese of Chicago.'"[56]

Thus Bishop Kozlowski and his local-universal church diocese in Chicago became the genesis of the church that would later be known as the Polish National Catholic Church. All Saints Catholic Church, in communion with Bishop Kozlowski, became the first *official* Old Catholic diocese in North America canonically in communion with the Union of Utrecht!

Similar occurrences like the All Saints incident in Chicago began surfacing in cities across the U.S. in the early nineteenth-century, where conflicts between the predominantly Irish Roman Catholic hierarchy and the Polish-American immigrants could not be resolved. For example, a similar incident occurred in Scranton, Pennsylvania, not long after Kozlowski was consecrated a bishop by the Union of Utrecht, where a Fr. Hodur began a ministry to Poles who had separated from the Roman church over property title and power controversies. Fr.

Hodur was considered by those closest to him as a complicated man. Orzell informs us that "Fr. Hodur...was ordained [a priest] at Scranton in 1893, was a very complex man whose radical rhetoric blended populism, nationalism, anti-clericalism, Catholicism and, initially, socialism into an attractive Church."[57] Fr. Hodur and Bishop Kozlowski did not see *eye-to-eye* on many issues, and were thus constantly at odds with each other. Hodur tried to seek consecration from the Union of Utrecht apart from Bishop Kozlowski, but the European Old Catholic bishops refused to consecrate him a bishop until he and Kozlowski worked something out on the local national level. To Hodur's benefit, Kozlowski died in January of 1907, and Hodur was unanimously voted as the succeeding bishop of the Polish Church by 25 parishes consisting of close to 80,000 communicants at that time across the U.S. Hodur was consecrated a bishop by the Union of Utrecht's college of bishops on September 29, 1907. That same year, he extended the name of his local church community in Scranton, PA to the entire national local Old Catholic church in America, calling it *The Polish National Catholic Church*.

At the peak of the PNCC's existence there were well over 100,000 communicants in the 1950s to the early 1980s. These numbers have since dwindled, and many PNCC parishes are currently struggling to remain open.[58] The PNCC's relationship with the Union of Utrecht has always been unstable because the PNCC struggled (much like the church of Utrecht) to distance itself from certain *Romish* devotions, i.e. the rosary and eucharistic adoration. These kinds of devotions were not embraced by the European churches of Utrecht; however, they did not prevent the

PNCC from celebrating what they deemed to be cultural and local devotions. In other words, the spiritual devotions practiced by the PNCC were, according to the European churches, not part of the *essentials* of the Catholic faith. The PNCC did not share this "local Church" mindset, and believed that

> Western European Old Catholic leaders, many of whom are disaffected, radical ex-Roman Catholics...have come under liberal Anglican influence as a result of their full communion with the Church of England under the terms of the Bonn Agreement (1931), actually hoped that the PNCC eventually would succumb to modernism (to maintain the Union between Europe and America).[59]

The main conflict between the PNCC and the European churches of the Union of Utrecht does not concern itself with the superfluous particularities of church discipline and morals as Orzell seems to believe,[60] rather the "principal cause" of the conflict is theological, how one views the nature of the church. It is clear that the PNCC practices a *universal ecclesiology* which is primarily embraced in the Western Church, especially the Roman Catholic Church. Universal ecclesiology "sees the whole church in the whole world as a single organic entity...,"[61] where local churches merely reflect in part the one universal church through its commonality and conformity in likeness to each other. Orthodox theologian and pioneer of eucharistic ecclesiology, Nicolas Afanasiev, informs us that,

118 | Robert W. Caruso

> ...universal ecclesiology is a product of the imperial mindset, which sees unity as derived from centralization.... Using Paul's image of the body of Christ, [early church theologian] Cyprian developed the idea that fullness and unity are attributes of the whole church, and each local manifestation is merely a member or part of that whole, not itself possessing catholicity. The Catholic Church is the sum of its parts, like the branches of a tree.... (Universal ecclesiology) was not the pattern of the primitive church.[62]

Roman Catholic scholar of church history, M. Edmund Hussey, provides a laconic synopsis of Nicolas Affanassiev's five essential elements in describing universal ecclesiology, they are: "the fullness of the church is in the universal church; local churches are a part of the universal church; universal ecclesiology logically leads to a doctrine of primacy, even if not necessarily a specifically Roman one."[63] Thus the understanding of *communion* from a universal ecclesiological paradigm is to be of like mind in faith, morals, and discipline as primarily decreed by one church, one bishop (e.g. the pope or patriarch), and one magisterium (teaching office of the Catholic Church) to its various local church parts throughout the world.

The churches of the Union of Utrecht reject *universal ecclesiology* and instead favor a more primitive view of the church known as *eucharistic ecclesiology*. Eucharistic ecclesiology of the early church strives to understand the universal church's fundamental nature as *koinonia* by patterning it after the communal likeness of the Triune God.

Eucharistic ecclesiology, unlike universal ecclesiology, finds its historical origins in the eucharistic theology of the early church of the first three centuries. Eucharistic ecclesiology is uniquely different from universal ecclesiology because it asserts that the universal church, in its wholeness, is always manifested in the particular local church united in the celebration of Eucharist with its local bishop throughout the world. In other words, the Eucharist and the local church are so interconnected that it becomes

> ...the primary manifestation of the church, containing within itself the fullness of the sacramental life. Consequently the eucharist is not merely a sacrament *of* the church in the sense that it is possessed and used by the church, but it is also a sacrament that is *constitutive of the church* in the sense that it truly incarnates or actualizes the church as the Christian community in a certain time and place.[64]

Because every local church seeks eucharistic communion with other local churches, each local church *fully contains the one Catholic Church* because it "[partakes] of the one loaf which is the body of Christ...gathered around a bishop [comprising] the fundamental unity of the church."[65] Authentic communion occurs in freedom and love amidst difference on the local level in eucharistic ecclesiology. As Afanassiev describes it, "the Church's oneness in local multiplicity is the essential vision of eucharistic ecclesiology."[66]

Clearly, the European Old Catholic churches have succeeded in "...maintaining close ties to Anglicans...and have entered into an intercommunion agreement with Lutherans…,"[67] because eucharistic ecclesiology does not mandate conformity, but rather hospitably looks for those *essential* characteristics that comprise what it means to be church. Suffice it to state here that the primary conflict that eventually caused the PNCC and the European Old Catholic churches to schism did not occur because of malice or manipulation by either side; it was just that both churches were working from two very different ecclesiological paradigms concerning the nature of the church. So, when the Old Catholic bishops "…from Austria, Germany, the Netherlands, and Switzerland made it clear that while they did not require the PNCC to adopt the ordination of women, the blessing of homosexual partnerships, or the practice of intercommunion with Protestants, they did expect it to lift virtually all restrictions on sacramental sharing with those who had done so."[68] It is clear in this statement that the European Old Catholic bishops embrace a more primitive *eucharistic ecclesiological* understanding of unity in diversity in how they viewed doctrinal essentials and its praxis on the local level of the church. The PNCC bishops struggled with the European Old Catholic bishops' ecclesiological views of allowing diversity to occur on the local church level in matters of discipline, because they, for the most part, embraced a *universal ecclesiological* understanding of the church where unity is located in the conformity on all matters of church faith and discipline.

The PNCC parted ways with the Union of Utrecht in 2003 because it refused to participate in a *full communion* status with Utrecht as described above.[69] The European churches of the Union of Utrecht with its college of bishops have always been adamant in stating that *full communion* is what they seek to achieve with other local churches. This will never occur between the Union of Utrecht and the PNCC so long as the PNCC's college of bishops continue to embrace a universal ecclesiological understanding of the church.[70] Laurence Orzell argues in his essay entitled *Disunion of Utrecht* that the European Old Catholic churches departed from the *classical* understanding of Old Catholic theological belief for a more modernized Protestant theology. He further claims in this essay that the "principal cause" of the split between the PNCC and the Union of Utrecht was over three very specific issues concerning women's ordination, homosexuality, and the pursuit of ecumenical relations with "Protestant churches." Orzell's main thesis in his essay seems a bit too simplistic and generalized in claiming that the Union of Utrecht "expelled the U.S.-based Polish National Catholic Church (PNCC)…, for being, in effect, too traditional."[71] This sort of polemic against the Union of Utrecht is much too simplistic, and Orzell fails to theologically observe and address the underlying ecclesiological problem that exists between the PNCC and the Union of Utrecht.

The Union of Utrecht has historically embraced a *eucharistic* rather than a *universal* understanding of the church. Meaning, there is nothing novel, modern, or liberal about how the Union of Utrecht sought to maintain communion with the PNCC. The Union of Utrecht's college of bishops, in union with its local synods, was merely working from an ecclesiology that emphasizes respect for local church autonomy so long as the *essentials* of the Christian faith are practiced (as delineated in the eight articles of the Declaration of Utrecht).

There is nothing in the Declaration of Utrecht that would prevent or advocate for the ordination of women to the ministerial priesthood, admitting homosexuals into the full life of the local body of Christ, or seek ecumenical fellowship with other Christian church denominations on the local level, because the *essentials* of the Christian faith of the first seven ecumenical councils remain unaffected. Further, prominent modern biblical scholarship has persuasively argued, to the chagrin of theologians like Orzell, that women *did* serve as deacons in the early church and homosexual relationships (not merely same-sex sexual activity) were a matter altogether unknown in the early church as well as in scripture. However, we must set this matter aside because it goes beyond our current study.[72]

In fact, Orzell's understanding of the Union of Utrecht's perceived progressivism is actually more eucharistic than innovative because the European Old Catholics truly believe that the local churches who "…[enter] into communion with one another"[73] on the local level are bound together and sealed in communion by the Holy Spirit in the essentials of the faith. It is not that the European Old Catholic churches succumbed to a more progressive or liberal understanding of the church, rather it exposes the PNCC's stubbornness and outright rejection of Old Catholic eucharistic ecclesiology in general. It is interesting to note here that Orzell's "all or nothing" thesis claim against the Union of Utrecht merely reinforces my original assertion that the underlying struggle between the PNCC and the Union of Utrecht was not so much about differing political beliefs (conservative versus liberal), as it was about altogether different approaches toward understanding the nature of the church.

The Polish National Catholic Church was the first and last U.S. ecclesial polity, apart from the Episcopal Church (USA), to be officially affiliated (in communion) with the Union of Utrecht. The PNCC has been trying to define its Catholic identity apart from the Old Catholic tradition as a viable mainstream church in America. This has proven to be a difficult endeavor considering that the number of PNCC communicants has dwindled significantly in the last twenty years, and their strong ethnocentric identity precludes non-Polish persons from ever considering membership in one of its parishes for the most part. Furthermore, the Catholic identity and character fostered by the PNCC is clearly more Roman Catholic than Old Catholic, but the PNCC currently belongs to neither communion.[74]

Again, as with Bishop Mathew, the Union of Utrecht's college of bishops moved too quickly in consecrating Fr. Kozlowski a bishop for the Polish immigrants in the U.S. That is, they did not carefully weigh the positive and negative affects such an action would have on the Union of Utrecht for years to come. This is not to suggest that the Union of Utrecht's bishops were irresponsible in either of the two cases mentioned above, it is merely an observation that the Union of Utrecht bishops moved too quickly in consecrating Fr. Kozlowski to the Old Catholic episcopacy. There is no doubt that the Union of Utrecht desired to form *koinonia* with the Polish immigrants in America who were perceived by its college of bishops to be a like-minded group of disaffected Roman Catholic laity and clergy who needed a bishop for their newly formed "emergency" local church. Only in this circumstance the confrontation between the Roman hierarchy and laity transpired on North American soil and not European. On the surface, the PNCC seemed to have been born out of a similar situation as the Union of Utrecht; however, a closer analysis of the situation uncovers a very different reality. If the Union of Utrecht's college of bishops had spent more time in discernment with the PNCC *before* forming *koinonia* with them, some of the conflicts described above might well have been avoided. Little to no time was given to serious theological dialogue, which in retrospect may have provided a clearer recognition by both groups as to whether or not they were of the same essence and character in being church. This type of "process recognition" can not be coerced or hastily rushed into, but rather seeks to foster relationships centered in freedom and love, an *establishment of communion in the power of the Holy Spirit!*

Concluding, the Polish National Catholic Church is a polity that shares in the overall complex history of the Old Catholic churches of the Union of Utrecht. It is unfortunate that a schism occurred between the PNCC and the European churches of the Union of Utrecht because divisions like this are always caused by human fallibility, and in turn, grieves the Holy Spirit.

II. The Contemporary Independent Old Catholic Groups in the United States of America: Authentic Movement or Façade for Unbridled Clericalism?

There are many ways to label the independent Old Catholic movement in the U.S., some are more positive than others. The purpose of this section is not to depict independent Old Catholicism in America in either a positive or negative light. Rather my intention here is to elucidate a clear and coherently realistic analysis of the U.S. independent Old Catholic groups as they currently exist today. Specifically, we will focus on some of the real dilemmas these groups face with regard to contemporary Old Catholic eucharistic ecclesiology.

The independent Old Catholic groups in North America (excluding the PNCC) tend to focus their distinctive theological, historical, and missional characters with that of bishops Mathew and Vilatte.[75] We already discovered in section one of this chapter that Mathew and Vilatte and their American contemporaries (e.g. Pruter, Queen, NeSmith, among others) teach a peculiar way of being "Old Catholic" in America "...that was not unlike the Roman Church in many of its *theological views, but different in its discipline.*"[76] According to this school of thought, church discipline becomes the primary instigator that forces individuals in America to schism with Rome. Specifically, the disciplinary issues I am referring to here tend to focus on money, property (e.g. the PNCC conflicts), or tolerating certain social moral values (i.e. homosexuality, divorce, abortion, contraception, et cetera).

The Union of Utrecht was born out of a *theological* crisis and moved from this historical event to try to *theologically* understand its Catholicity apart from the Roman Catholic Church. The result was that the Union of Utrecht, through its theologians, re-discovered the dynamic and transformative "catholic" theology of the early church; a theology that encompasses both eastern *and* western ideas about God, Eucharist, and the nature of the church. Generally speaking, early church theology of the first three-centuries was quite different (dare I say antithetical?) from the post-Trentian medieval scholasticism (i.e. Thomas Aquinas) of the Roman Catholic Church. Moreover, Patristic theology has greatly influenced even the most contemporary ideas in Roman Catholic theology and ecclesiology today.[77] The independent Old Catholic groups in America had no such theological revolution like that of the Union of Utrecht. Meaning, most of the contemporary American independent Old Catholic groups are (for the most part) theologically and ecclesiologically *compatible* with their Roman Catholic counterparts. The point to be made here, for better or for worse, is that the American and European Old Catholics were born out of two very different theological and historical contexts, and the differences (theologically speaking) are strikingly obvious in many ways to most reasonable minds.

The above theological differences (although a challenge for both groups) really do not touch upon the main issue that has eroded the vitality and growth of the U.S. independent Old Catholics that claim to share in the Vilatte and/or Mathew historical line of apostolic succession. The dilemma I allude to is the impending problem of an "accommodating clericalism" that tends to permeate the overall identity of independent Old Catholicism on the local level. There are two general, yet realistic facts that most U.S. independent Old Catholic groups need to face if there is truly a desire to form *koinonia* with other chuches. They are: (1) most American independent Old Catholic communities are composed of clergy and bishops who were once Roman Catholic (lay or already ordained) and left the Roman communion for reasons too numerous to list here; and (2), there is minimal laity involvement and very small, close to non-existent, parishes on the local level.[78] This accommodating clerical mentality is exuded by most of the U.S. independent bishops and their priests, who tend to saturate the overall character of independent Old Catholics in many ways. For instance, most independent Old Catholic bishops continue to randomly ordain individuals to the priesthood across the U.S. who are ill-qualified (academically, spiritually, and sometimes psychologically) and are often motivated by their own self-interest; indeed these actions foster a clericalized idea that ministry *primarily* finds its genesis in the sacramental ranks of Holy Orders and *not* in the sacrament of Baptism. Further, most U.S. independent Old Catholic bishops function in a highly individualized manner and, as previously stated, do not exude a collegial respect for each others' authority on the local level.

Often times self-labeled Old Catholic bishops in the U.S. function as "supra-bishops" by ordaining individuals to the independent priesthood and episcopate all over the country as though the entire nation was their diocese. Bishops of this sort possess no sensibility of constraint in establishing reasonable geographical boundaries for their local church. For example, California is a very large state with millions of people, so why are local bishops in California establishing parishes in Florida? It makes no sense and just reinforces the lack of deference for other bishops and their local churches. But even this statement is misleading because most of the independent Old Catholic bishops do not serve a "local-universal church."[79] Meaning, most independent Old Catholic bishops have no laity on the local level that gather around and recognize him as *their bishop*!

Most of the independent Old Catholic groups in America consist of priests gathered around the bishop who recognize him as *their bishop*! Where some small independent local-universal churches actually do exist in the U.S., there is great confusion in understanding their ecclesial character and identity as Old Catholics, which is due mostly to a lack of resources and ill-qualified/educated clergy. In these small independent local-universal churches there is a real noticeable absence of conciliarism (shared authority) between the laity, clergy, and the bishop. Meaning, there is great reluctance on the part of the independent Old Catholic clergy and bishops toward understanding the *theological* concepts of conciliarism that leads the local baptized (the *laos*) beyond mere ecclesiastical protocol to a different way of *theologically* understanding the nature of the church; a nature of the local catholic church that is *not* primarily hierarchical and/or institutional, but is engaged in *being as communion* on the local level, what I deem the *koinonia* church.

The *koinonia* church is purely organic, local, and relational. It finds its being and missional purpose in the communal personhood of Christ constituted in the power of the Holy Spirit. If eucharistic ecclesiology is to have any merit or meaning whatsoever, it needs to become a lived teaching! That is, bishops need to be able to *pastorally* relate not just to their priests but also to their laity! Authority is something that is shared and not possessed by any one part of the body of Christ on the local level. Meaning, it is the laity and clergy in communion with the bishop on the local level that govern the local church universal together in freedom and love. So, for instance, the bishop cannot solely act as his own authority without being held accountable to the rest of the local church and the same goes for the laity as well as the clergy. We are all trusted servants of one another, and no one individual or group governs Christ's local church in its entirety! I have yet to see an independent Old Catholic bishop in this country honestly strive to implement the eucharistic ecclesiology of the local catholic church because it would mean (among other things) a paradigmatic transformation in how one understands power and authority as existing, not *just* with the clergy and the bishop, but also *with* the laity in a sharing of mutuality centered in hospitality, humility, freedom, and most of all love. Further, this would mean that lay involvement would have to increase and invest a more active role in their community. It is imperative that Old Catholic laity become the catalysts in helping to form the identity of the church they claim to *be* on the local level.

Anglican liturgist, Richard Giles, poignantly emphasizes the conciliar shared authority characteristic of eucharistic ecclesiology through the eucharistic liturgy (the Holy Mass—the source and summit of our Catholic spiritual life together) by liturgically describing the ancient idea of prayer as the measure of one's belief (Latin: *lex orendi, lex credendi*). He tells us,

> For centuries, clergy and laity have colluded in a deal to keep alive the Levitical habits of priest-hood because it is convenient for both camps: the clergy are kept in a job with a good pension, and the laity can offload all responsibilities to the priestly caste separated out from among them. It is high time we undid this cozy deal.

One way of challenging this historic conspiracy in the liturgy [including the entire life of the local-universal church] is to take the highly significant step of reducing to one the number of stoles worn, no matter how many clergy are leading worship.... In this way the stole becomes the stole of the assembly. It is worn by the presiding minister, as conductor of the orchestra, and then given in turn to any member of the assembly called forth to play a solo part in making the music of the liturgy. So then the reader, the deacon, the preacher, the intercessor, the cantor, will each in turn come to the presiding minister to receive the stole before they play their part. In this way we make absolutely explicit the priestly nature and shared ministry [established in the sacrament of baptism] of the *whole assembly* [the local-universal body of Christ].

In so doing of course the presiding minister [bishop or presbyter] in no way loses authority, but in fact enhances it. For in the true spirit of the gospel, he/she relinquishes power in order to exercise it more nobly and humbly in a true act of *noblesse oblige*.[80]

The independent Old Catholic bishops and priests of this country have yet to fully embrace this *noblesse oblige*[81] understanding of the church because, if they did, they would reject individual notions of power, privilege, and an egotistical sense of being distinctive or special in the church. Eucharistic ecclesiology provides a different understanding of being in *persona Christi* (in the person of

Christ) that many of the independent Old Catholic bishops and clergy struggle to fully comprehend and embrace. It is, however, one of the foundational characteristics of Old Catholic ecclesiology, and a failure to fully embrace and actualize this characteristic (of being as communion) is a failure to live up to the name of the church the independent groups affiliate themselves with! The fact remains that American independent Old Catholic bishops and priests, until they fully relinquish their embedded clericalism, will continue to struggle with comprehending Old Catholic eucharistic ecclesiology, which constitutes mission and ministry in all the baptized (the *laos*) and not just the local ordained priestly ministry of Word and Sacrament.

A. The Eucharistic Nature of the Old Catholic Priesthood

How is the ordained priesthood understood within the context of eucharistic ecclesiology? The character of Old Catholic eucharistic ecclesiology emphasizes the necessity of *communion and relatedness* between the bishop and the laity in forming church on the local-universal level, but it also gives the impression that the ordained priesthood (a.k.a. the ministerial priesthood) is, by definition, not necessary when forming local church. Why is that? Is not the ministerial presbyterate one of the foundational characteristics of what defines the local catholic church? The short answer to the latter question is no, the ordained ministerial presbyterate is *not a foundational characteristic of what defines the local-universal church*. Communion and relationship is the foundational ethos that forms the body of Christ on the local level. In other words, the early churches of the first three centuries viewed "local church" as the laity gathered around the eucharistic *charisma* of the local bishop. During this time in history the Greek words *presbyteros* and *episkopé* generally referred to one and the same person: the bishop.[82] Episcopal theologian, James M. Barnett, has convincingly asserted that presbyters *did exist* in apostolic times by referencing Acts 20 and 21. In his book, Barnett informs us that the rank of presbyter was so intimately connected to that of the bishop that its role was always eclipsed by the role of the bishop.[83] I concur with Barnett here that the rank of presbyter did indeed exist in the early church; however, I want to also re-assert that the presbyter was and is not a *foundational element* in defining the local-universal church. According to Zizioulas, the ancient roles of presbyter and bishop were so intimately related in the primitive church that no separation between the two existed. The presbyter's ministry in the early church was always a reflection of the ministry of the *episkop* (overseer) in the context of the celebration of Eucharist.[84] The early church of the first three-centuries was *episcopocentric* and not *presbyterocentric*.[85] It was only later in the early fourth-century that the word *parish* began to surface in Rome and with that the separation of the word *presbyteros* (elder, later known as "priest") from *episkopé* (bishop or "overseer"). Thus, even though contemporary scholarship cannot pinpoint exactly when the parish and the ordained ministry of the presbyterate (as being a separate rank in ordained ministry from that of the bishop) occurred, Zizioulas asserts that evidence of such language begins to surface in Rome in the early 300s.[86]

The role of the presbyter began to form an identity of its own sometime in the late fourth-century onward apart from the rank of the episcopacy. Old Catholic eucharistic ecclesiology emphasizes this early church *relational* character of the presbytery as being a distinguishable rank apart from the bishop, but is still at the same time intimately *related* or connected to the *charisma* of the local bishop. The presbyter should be understood as the icon of the local bishop, and uniquely shares in the episcopal *charisma* of being *in persona Christi* (in the person of Christ) to and for the local parish communities of the laity in the celebration of the Eucharist on the local level. Having made this assertion, we must remain ever-vigilant as to how the Latin phrase *in persona Christi* is used to describe the ordained ministry, so to avoid a *Romish-like* medieval clericalism that to this day permeates the Roman Catholic church.[87] This type of clericalism found in the Roman church fosters a privileged mentality among ordained presbyters as being the sole "dispensers" and "guardians" of the local church's sacramental grace; this clerical mindset has no place in Old Catholic eucharistic ecclesiology.[88] The Old Catholic churches of the Union of Utrecht do not foster this kind of privileged clericalism, rather Old Catholics prefer an ecclesiology that fosters communion, which leads to mission through the diverse gifts of the baptized *working and relating together* in freedom and love on the local level.

The Old Catholic ministerial prebyterate is intimately connected with presiding at the celebration of Eucharist, where the fullness of Christ's priesthood is not located in any one individual but in the gathered assembly of all the baptized. Accordingly then, the presbyter primarily possesses a liturgical identity as *offering the eucharistic gifts on behalf of the bishop, representing the totality of Christ's priesthood in the celebration of Eucharist with the gathered local body of Christ.* This "offering" identity is ascribed to the presbyter because it was related to his liturgical role in the early church's Divine Liturgy as attested to in Hippolytus' *Apostolic Tradition.* According to Zizioulas, "...the Bishop [has] the function of offering the gifts by right of his ordination [and] enjoins a certain sort of active participation by the Presbyters at the sacred moment of the blessing and offering of the Eucharist performed by the bishop...."[89] This interpretation of Hippolytus' text informs us that (a) the presbyterate is intimately related to the local episcopacy, and (b) the presbyterate finds its primary identity in the liturgical offering of the eucharistic gifts (Christ's body and blood) with the laity in the power of the Holy Spirit, giving all thanks and glory to God the Father of all creation.[90] Hence, "...in a eucharistic ecclesiology, the ministry [of the ordained presbyter] is understood to be primarily the service of presiding over the gathering of the whole people of God in such a way that all charisms are enabled to contribute their part to the whole."[91]

Old Catholic eucharistic ecclesiology views Eucharist as the core *being* of the local catholic church because all grace, faith, hope, and love comes from *being as communion* in Christ's person who sustains and nourishes the baptized in the power of the Holy Spirit.[92] The ordained priestly ministerial *ranks* of deacon, presbyter, and bishop are first and foremost Christ's ministry because it is he who is head servant, priest, and shepherd of every local-universal church throughout the world. Aside from the royal priesthood of the baptized, Christ, in the power of the Holy Spirit, established through His apostles the sacramental priestly ministry of the one Holy Order in three *equal* ranks of deacon, priest, and bishop.[93] These three *mysterious* ranks of Holy Order *serve* Christ's mystical body on earth in giving all praise, thanksgiving, and joy to God the Father for giving us the only-begotten Son in communion with the Holy Spirit. Specifically, the presbyter's life and work is not hers alone, but that of Christ's. There is no ontological change bestowed upon an individual at ordination, nor is the ordained presbyter solely a *function* within the local catholic church. Instead, through the laying on of hands by the bishop, the ordained presbyter is given an indelible (permanent) charism of *being a relational entity* of Christ's communal personhood centered in the power of the Spirit. The indelible character bestowed upon a presbyter at ordination is thus a gift of *koinonia* (communion), a gift of *sacramental* ministry that fosters and upholds the eucharistic essence of the local-universal church's communion as unity in diversity centered in love. Zizioulas plainly attests to this *koinonia* charism of the presbyter when he states, "Ordination and ministry as communion are precisely and *only* describable in terms of love."[94] That is, love binds, nourishes, and serves to describe all that is *koinonia* in the diverse local body of Christ, and the ordained presbyter shares (with the local bishop) in this indelible *charisma* of selfless communion, which is always centered in love and freedom for and towards the *other* (1 Cor.13).[95]

This means, among other things, that presbyters *must not clericalize the eucharistic liturgy*! It is not the presbyter who alone "says or celebrates the mass." Rather, it is the gathered priestly assembly who concelebrate the eucharistic mysteries together *with* the presbyter who is the presiding minister of the Holy Mass. All ministers of the eucharistic liturgy, not *just* the presbyter, serve the gathered priestly assembly of the baptized in fulfilling communion with each other and God. In the celebration of Christ's paschal mystery at Mass the gathered priestly assembly, through its equal yet diverse gifts of ministry, together manifest the Blessed Sacrament of Christ's body and blood in a most real, true, and effective manner. The indelible *charisma* of the presbyter is communion centered in the eucharistic nature of the church manifested in the celebration of Eucharist, which is by its very essence a communal event! This means that the days of the presbyter *saying* Mass alone apart from a gathered assembly must come to an end because such an action is antithetical to the eucharistic nature of communion. That is, it denies the *koinonia charisma* of the presbyterate by emphasizing an individual *sacerdotal* power apart from the communion of the eucharistic fellowship of the local-universal church. The presbyter, and all the ordained, are "designated to serve the [gathered] assembly's needs,"[96] and not just one's own *clericalized* egocentric sense of importance. Hence the rank of presbyter in the sacrament of Holy Order is not one of honor or uniqueness as a *status* within Christ's mystical body on earth, but one of necessity to serve and strengthen the body through Word and Sacrament, as well as show forth the essence of Christ's personhood—which is communion centered in love for the other as well as for one's self.

Conclusion

This section has tried to elucidate a clear and coherently realistic analysis of the U.S. independent Old Catholic groups as they exist today. Specifically, we focused on some of the real dilemmas independent Old Catholic groups in North America face with regard to contemporary Old Catholic eucharistic ecclesiology. The ministry of the presbyter (a/k/a the ordained priest) is an important ministry of the local church universal, and formation for the ordained presbyterate should be conducted in a responsible reasonable manner. American independent Old Catholic bishops must require and insure that their local presbyters are properly trained in a reputable and accredited academic seminary environment that is not antithetical towards Old Catholic theological discourse. Every local church, in union with its local bishop, must strive to produce above average ordained ministers of Word and Sacrament!

It is senseless when some independent Old Catholic bishops immediately ordain and/or accept (incardinate) persons of other denominations (this includes persons from the Roman Catholic Church) to the ranks of deacon or presbyter *before* he or she has lived, breathed, and practiced the Old Catholic faith within a *viable* Old Catholic parish community on the local level.[97] Further stated, just because a person was a Roman Catholic (or ordained a priest in the Roman tradition) does not *ipso facto* determine that she or he is qualified to be an ordained minister in an Old Catholic local church. The independent Old Catholic groups must learn to distance themselves from the *Prutarian* school of thought—that Old Catholicism is a pseudo-type of Roman Catholicism. The Old Catholic

Church possesses a different and rich theological tradition apart from the Roman church as explicated above.

There is no doubt that the church needs highly trained, passionate, intelligent, and dedicated ordained deacons and presbyters who are capable of serving the needs of the local church universal. This means time, energy, and financial investment is required of the candidate seeking ordination. The allotted periods of time throughout the formation process allows the candidate, as well as the local bishop, to discern whether or not he or she is truly called to the ordained ministry of presbyter. *Presbyters do not form parishes*, the laity in communion with their bishop do! The accepted practice by many independent Old Catholic bishops in the U.S. is to ordain as many presbyters as possible, so they can in turn form parishes on their behalf. Essentially this is a hierarchal, top-down church paradigm that emphasizes the idea that *local church* is formed and created by the clergy in communion with a bishop. In this model of local church it is acceptable to create parishes with little to non-existent lay involvement. That is, in a typical U.S. independent Old Catholic church community a "parish" is defined as a priest renting space in a "mainline" Protestant/Reformed church building, where he or she "sets up shop" to *say Mass* with the hope that some laity might come every Sunday to worship with him or her. More often than not, the priest pays for the worship space out of his or her own pocket with the hope that a couple of dollars will be placed in the donation basket to help with the rental expenses. It is obvious to the reasonable mind that this is not the way parish communities form, and clergy who practice church in this dysfunctional and highly clerical manner will not be taken seriously by most laity, nor experience any significant growth in the parish itself.

American independent Old Catholic clergy and bishops have successfully objectified the laity as consumers of religion. Relationship and communion is, at best, superficial in that there is no responsibility or expectation placed on either the clergy or laity. Most lay persons who attend independent Old Catholic Masses do so out of convenience to consume what the independent priest offers: the sacraments. This practice demeans both the rank of the presbyter and the order of the *laos* in general. There are no formal systems of structure and responsibility in most independent Old Catholic parishes, and the priest makes part of his or her living working a secular job and dispensing sacramental rites for a fee (e.g., weddings, funerals, baptisms, etc.). These facts have essentially formed the independent Old Catholic clergy into being sacramental dispensers of *cheap grace*, and tend to perpetuate the overall dysfunctional character of the independent Old Catholic groups in North America.[98] No more should independent Old Catholic bishops and clergy sell the sacraments to Roman Catholic laity! No more should the Roman Catholic laity take advantage of the egos of the independent Old Catholic clergy for their own advantage! Old Catholic clergy are not *sacramental mills* for Roman Catholic laity.

Lastly, the independent Old Catholic bishops and clergy have a responsibility to learn about the church they claim to be. This means that much of what is currently accepted and practiced as being "Old Catholic" in the U.S. can no longer be accommodated, but 1) authentically realized as being something other than Old Catholic, and 2) begin a paradigmatic transformation of what it means to be Old Catholic in the U.S. through proper education and shared power and responsibility with the laity on the local level. If Old Catholicism is to have the potential of becoming an authentic movement in the U.S., the ordained ministry of deacon, presbyter, and bishop needs to be understood as an enriching, yet difficult lifestyle; a lifestyle that should not be entered into casually but intentionally as one who is intimately connected to the local body of the baptized. The ordained (equal yet different) ranks of ministry in the sacrament of Holy Order is not so much to *set apart* as it is to amalgamate, in a most intimate and relational manner, the ministries of deacon, presbyter, bishop, and *laos* into the mystery of the local church universal's eucharistic spiritual lifestyle.

CHAPTER FOUR:
The Bonn Agreement of 1931

THE BONN AGREEMENT OF 1931 is the extraordinary communion agreement between the Old Catholic churches of the Union of Utrecht and the Anglican Communion. Unfortunately, this seventy-five year old ground-breaking communion agreement is still widely unknown among many Episcopalians (lay and clergy) in North America. The tides are changing though and a stronger awareness of Old Catholicism is beginning to surface in its sister local-universal churches of North America: the Episcopal Church (USA). This chapter endeavors to illuminate the three principles that formed the Bonn Agreement. They are: *doctrinal unity, mutual recognition, and independent co-operation.*[1] We will tersely analyze each of these principles separately, so to better comprehend why the Bonn agreement is of crucial importance to both the study of Old Catholic eucharistic ecclesiology and its ongoing relationship with the Anglican Communion.

A. Doctrinal Unity

The Bonn Agreement of 1931 is significant because it is the first concordance of communion that has ever expressed full unity between a Catholic church and a church born out of the sixteenth-century Protestant Reformation: the church of England/Anglican Communion. The Old Catholic churches of the Union of Utrecht have always understood themselves as a "bridge church" in reuniting the Catholic and Protestant/Reformed churches of the West. Although Old Catholics have always been numerically small, their presence is ecumenically significant because, as Moss writes,

> They are a true "bridge church" (more so than the Anglican Communion to which the name has been applied). They bear witness that it is possible to be Latin or "Western" Catholics without being Ultramontane [Roman Catholic]; they resemble the Roman Communion in their liturgy and law, the Orthodox Communion in their creed, the Anglican Communion in their theological position, and the Continental Protestants in their Teutonic [Germanic] mentality.[2]

Central to the Old Catholic ecumenical identity is its eucharistic ecclesiology of the local-universal church. That is, Old Catholics do not view the "Catholic Church" in any other way but locally. Communion and fellowship in the mystical body of Christ is always fully manifested in the local episcopal ministry and the gathered assembly in the celebration of Eucharist in the Holy Mass in *koinonia* with other local catholic churches throughout the world. This third-century patristic understanding on the eucharistic nature of the church has greatly assisted the Union of Utrecht and the Anglican Communion in recognizing their shared characteristics as "Church" in this regard. Moreover, this early church recognition is the foundation on which the *Bonn Agreement of 1931* was constructed.

One must not take for granted that it took practically an entire century (eighty years) of theological discourse and debates between Old Catholics and Anglicans before the Bonn Agreement was realized.[3] The Old Catholics and the Anglicans have always acknowledged, even as early as 1851, that if a communion between them was to occur, then much work and energy would have to be dedicated to the endeavor. There were many Anglican and Old Catholic theologians in the late nineteenth century who earnestly wanted to see their two churches reach full communion status, but did not live to see it occur. The behavior exuded by these theologians is commendable because their drive and commitment was not so much focused on the final result(s) of their work, but more on actively striving to fulfill Christ's prayer for unity in the church. Truly these theologians were God's instruments in the process of forming communion between Anglicans and Old Catholics.[4]

The Union of Utrecht chose to remain faithful to the ancient councils and early church eucharistic ecclesiology of Western Catholicism, as opposed to the sixteenth-century Protestant Reformation or the more novel twentieth-century "universal Pontifical ecclesiology" of the Roman Catholic Church.[5] Most North American independent Old Catholic clergy, bishops, and others continue to try to diminish the clear doctrinal difference between Rome and Utrecht. Moss provides convincing evidence that attempts to diminish the theological differences between the Old Catholics and Roman Catholics since the late nineteenth-century stating,

> Attempts have been made to show that the difference between the Old Catholics and Rome is not very great, after all; that it is confined to the dogmas of the Vatican Council, and that the Old Catholics hope, if these dogmas can be explained or modified, to return some day to the Roman obedience.[6]

Further, this act of justification mirrors not so much that of Old Catholicism, but more the incessant need by the North American independent Old Catholic clergy to seek validation from Rome for their very existence. Moss clarifies this confusion by stating that

> Nothing could be further from the truth. The Old Catholics reject, not only the dogmas of the Vatican Council, but the authority of the Council of Trent, and the Papal Supremacy, with all that follows from it. They do not regard the Pope as their patriarch; they do not pray for him by name in any of their rites. They differ from Rome in ethics and discipline, as well as in dogma: and they regard the special [infallible] Roman dogmas as "unchristian, uncatholic, impossible, and mischievous." There are, of course, different opinions among them on the subject, but there is no Romanizing party, and no one, as far as I know, who thinks that reunion with Rome is practicable.[7]

From its inception, the Union of Utrecht re-examined its Catholic identity apart from seeking any kind of validation from the Roman communion. This offered a sense of clarity and freedom for the Union of Utrecht to describe its Catholicity apart from Rome, and further opened the doors toward unity with other local-universal churches throughout the world, e.g., the Anglican Communion.[8]

The ever-flourishing ecumenical relationship between the Union of Utrecht and the Anglican Communion in the late nineteenth-century reached a new plateau at the Old Catholic Union Conference at Bonn, Germany in 1874. The Old Catholic leaders convoked this conference "…specifically for the purpose of promoting reunion, these were informal and unofficial conferences of theologians from various churches but primarily Anglican and Old Catholic."[9] The Bonn conference of 1874 should not be underestimated or overlooked because it is at this meeting that the Old Catholics and Anglicans become *theologically* aware of each other and their shared existence as local-universal churches. The fourteen theological theses' of agreement (known as the *Bonn Theses of 1874*)[10] were produced at this conference, offering for the first time written evidence of a shared consensus between Old Catholic and Anglican theologians on a variety of general theological topics. Systematically speaking, the Bonn theses delineates Anglican and Old Catholic theological agreement in the following areas of revelation: in both scripture *and* tradition as possessing equal authority in the life of the Church (Bonn 1874, no. 1-3, and 9), sacramentology (Bonn 1874, no. 8, and 11), justification and salvation (Bonn 1874, no. 5-7, and 12), and the eucharistic ecclesiology of the local-universal church (Bonn 1874, no. 4, 8b, 9b, 10, 13-14).[11]

According to Wright, the conference also adopted an agreement apart from the fourteen Bonn theses to remove the *Filioque* clause from the Nicene-Constantinople creed. The *Filioque's* underlying controversial claim is that the Spirit proceeds from the Father *and* the Son. This is a purely Western trinitarian theological assertion, having its theological origin found in Augustine of Hippo's book *On the Trinity*, where the Spirit is described as being the love between the Father and the Son. The Spirit is further described as an ancillary to Christ in accomplishing God's salvific work in creation. Augustine's theological assertion on the Trinity made it difficult to distinguish the unique relationship of the persons of the Trinity, and obscured the personhood of the Father as the only unoriginate origin from which the eternal breath of the Holy Spirit comes forth in properly establishing the ever generate Word of life in freedom and most of all in love. When the Western church inserted the *Filioque* clause into the Nicene-Constantinopolitan Creed (381) at the fourth council of Constantinople (869-70), the Eastern church did not agree with this action and refused to recognize the council's hasty decision as being ecumenically binding on their local catholic churches.[12] Accordingly, the Bonn conference of 1874 issued a joint statement of agreement concerning this ninth-century controversy stating:

> We agree that the way in which the Filioque was inserted into the Nicene Creed was illegal, and that, with a view to future peace and unity, it is much to be desired that the whole Church should set itself seriously to consider whether the Creed could possibly be restored to its primitive form, without sacrifice of any true doctrine

which is expressed in the present Western form.[13]

The Old Catholic churches of the Union of Utrecht are unanimous in rejecting the *Filioque* clause in the Nicene Creed, more so than the Anglicans. It is only natural that the Old Catholics would lay a special emphasis in rejecting the *Filioque* clause because its trinitarian and eucharistic ecclesiology compels it to do so. Much in the same way history compelled the Anglican Communion to emphasize that scripture contains all things necessary for salvation. Both these theological statements are true and faithful to the early church ecumenical councils' teaching, and they do not contradict each other in any way.[14]

There is much theological agreement between the Old Catholics and Anglicans as evidenced above, more so than with the Roman Catholic Church. The Bonn theses of 1874 provided a sturdy theological foundation for Old Catholics and Anglicans to stand on as they dove deeper into the murky waters of studying each others' ecclesiology. The theology of the nature of the church, known as ecclesiology, is one of the major barriers toward realizing full unity in the churches of the West because the theologies produced during the Protestant Reformation and the Roman Catholic Counter-Reformation in the sixteenth-century were created to be antithetical toward one another. The Bonn theses of 1874 provided the theological room necessary for Old Catholic and Anglican theologians to focus intently on one another's ecclesiology, which ultimately led to the mutual recognition of standards of communion as expressed in the 1931 Bonn Agreement.

B. Mutual Recognition

Old Catholic and Anglican theologians were keenly aware that before a canonical communion between their two churches could occur, they had to face each others' teachings on the nature of the Church. Meaning, both church traditions had to clearly explain to the other its theological understanding on the nature of the one, holy, catholic, and apostolic Church. Generally speaking, this is the work of ecclesiology and it is a daunting task because its ideas must take into account the existent structure and ministry of the institutional church. Thus great care was taken by both sides as they moved beyond the theology explicated in the Bonn theses of 1874 and ventured into the fragile topic of ecclesiology in the early twentieth-century.

The 1874 Bonn theses acknowledged, among other things, that the Church of England, "and the churches derived through her" (Bonn 1874, no. 9), is indeed part of the unbroken line of apostolic succession. This late nine-teenth-century theological statement of agreement between the churches of the Union of Utrecht (except the Church of Utrecht)[15] and the Anglican Communion was the foundational first step toward recognizing a mutual ecclesiology and a shared three-fold ordained ministry of bishop, presbyter, and deacon centered in equality and love. Both churches were comfortable enough to recognize the validity of each others' ordained ministry in the Bonn Theses because the foundational basis of most of their theological doctrines was based in the primitive church of the first ten centuries. Meaning, Anglicans and Old Catholics have a clear sense of shared identity, in that the nature of the church is a eucharistic fellowship, where *koinonia* (communion) is the ontologically constitutive element in describing the iconic nature and mission of the church in relationship to the Father through Christ in the power of the Holy Spirit.[16] Anglican theologians today express openness and a need towards further clarifying the ecclesiology of their own communion by trying to model a eucharistic and baptismal ecclesiology of the early church.[17]

The Anglican Lambeth Conference of 1930 met to discuss, among other things, the possibility of forming full communion with the Union of Utrecht. After much dialog with Old Catholic and Anglican theologians alike, the conference concluded, stating that they "...agree that there is *nothing* in the Declaration of Utrecht inconsistent with the teaching of the Church of England."[18] The conference at Bonn took place a year after the 1930 Lambeth statement. Official delegates from both churches met at Bonn in 1931 and focused primarily on the question of ecclesiological recognition and whether a full communion agreement was possible. Clearly, both church communions were *episcopocentric*, but how did each communion understand the apostolic character of the episcopacy? Was ordained ministry simply an appointed function or was it a special gift of the Spirit? The Old Catholics were asking these questions from a eucharistic ecclesiological perspective, and they wondered whether the Anglicans were in communion with this constitutive understanding of the church. The concern here was whether or not the two churches practiced a mutual apostolic understanding of the church. The Anglican delegates replied affirmatively, stating:

>...they [the Anglican Communion] all believed
>that the Holy Spirit was given in ordination for
>the work of the ministry... The Old Catholics
>were satisfied that all members of the Anglican
>Communion regarded their Church as continu-
>ous from the pre-Reformation Church, and
>therefore different from communions which had
>no history beyond the sixteenth-century; and
>this was what they (the Old Catholics) wanted to
>know.[19]

After much dialogue and effort at both the 1874 and
1931 Bonn meetings Anglicans and Old Catholics could
not but recognize their mutuality of catholicity and apostolicity in the doctrinal essentials of the other. Hence, the
Bonn Agreement of 1931 was created and a mutual recognition of *full communion* was at last a reality between
Anglicans and Old Catholics of the Union of Utrecht!

Implicit in the 1931 Bonn agreement is the eucharistic
ecclesiological character of the local-universal church.
The primary emphasis in the 1931 Bonn Agreement is the
communal fellowship of sharing in the very life and ministry of Christ's historical body manifested in the power of
the Spirit through the communal celebration of the
Eucharist.[20] This echoes St. Ignatius' assertion that "...the
Church is the body of Christ because the body of Christ
is *the historical Christ Himself* and the historical Christ is
the flesh of the Divine Eucharist. The local Church, then, is
the *whole Church* for no other reason than because *the
whole historical Christ* is made incarnate within her
through the Divine Eucharist."[21] St. Ignatious is clear that
each local church is complete in itself because Christ is
made fully and really present in the unity of the local body

of Christ in the celebration of Eucharist, which "…at the same time…make[s] possible the common life and witness of all local churches in a universal conciliar fellowship"[22] of the one, holy, catholic, and apostolic Church in the world. It was further reasoned at Bonn that admittance to full participation in the sacramental life of each other's communion meant full acceptance and co-operation in all other areas of the church.[23] Thus, the Bonn Agreement of 1931 explicitly expresses an ecumenical ecclesiology of the Church as "…a eucharistic communion of local-universal churches,"[24] throughout the world centered in the mission and witness of the gospel.

C. Independent Co-operation

There is little doubt that the implicit eucharistic ecclesiology of the 1931 Bonn Agreement is what makes it a profound document of communion. Dr. Lukas Vischer, Swiss Protestant theologian and ecumenist, stated in a lecture in the early 1980s that the Bonn Agreement was an instrument of real progress in the ecumenical movement because it contained an implicit eucharsitic ecclesiology; he further acknowledged that the Bonn Agreement, "is both an invitation and a criticism within the ecumenical movement: an invitation to the Churches to return to the tradition of the early Church and a criticism of the Churches for having abandoned this tradition by exaggerating the authority of the hierarchy, especially the authority of the Pope, or by weakening the allegiance to the heritage of the early Church."[25] Each local church is united and independent from all other local churches by virtue of its lived eucharistic fellowship centered in the total mystery of Christ's real and unending presence, yet each local church is also simultaneously universal (*Catholic*) because, as Zizioulas writes,

> It is in the nature of the eucharist to transcend not only divisions occurring within a local situation but also the very division which is inherent in the concept of geography: the division of the world into local places. Just as a eucharist which is not a transcendence of divisions within a certain locality is a false eucharist, equally a eucharist which takes place in conscious and intentional isolation and separation from other local communities in the world is not a true eucharist. From that it follows inevitably that a local Church, in order to be not just local but also Church, must be in full communion with the rest of the local Churches in the world.[26]

Thus, independence (or freedom) and universality coincide with each other relationally and communally in the bonds of love explicitly on the local level. Again, the Bonn Agreement testifies, although imperfectly, to this definition of the nature of the church.

Zizioulas informs us that the Catholic Church is both local and diverse simultaneously and should be primarily understood in this way.[27] The universal nature of the church should not overpower its local character, because it is precisely on the local level that we understand the church to be both local *and* universal at the same time in the celebration of Eucharist. This sort of illumination can only occur through an authentic communion between local-universal churches. The question that begs to be answered here is what does "authentic communion" mean? From a eucharistic ecclesiological perspective it means that every local-universal church is aware of the problems and concerns of *not only their church* but also with all other churches throughout the world; it means that every local-universal church should possess a common and essential character with all other local-universal churches centered in the eucharistic mystery; and finally structures like the Bonn Agreement need to be created and implemented to help create and sustain universal fellowship between local churches.[28] It is here that the Bonn Agreement has not lived up to its eucharistic nature of "authentic communion" between the Anglicans and Old Catholics because both sides have failed to fully comprehend the communal vision and nature of the Catholic Church as it has been expressed above.

Vischer offers us a well reasoned and keen critique of some of the language used in the Bonn Agreement as sounding more like an *intercommunion* agreement than a *communion* agreement, which contradicts its implicit eucharistic ecclesiological nature. Specifically, Vischer directs our attention to the first clause in the agreement and acknowledges that each local church is independent as well as universal (Catholic) by virtue of its communal relationship with other local churches; however, Vischer correctly questions some of the language used in the first clause which states that each local church "maintain its own catholicity and independence" apart from the rest. There is an inherent contradiction with this statement found in the first clause of the agreement in relation to the last two clauses, which is implicitly eucharistic in nature. I believe it necessary to quote Vischer's comment on this issue of the 1931 Bonn Agreement's first clause, so to better understand the assertion introduced here. He states:

> It has to be said that, in certain respects, the
> [Bonn] agreement does not correspond but
> rather contradicts the vision of the Church
> which is the deepest inspiration of the two tradi-
> tions. This I need to explain. The agreement
> establishes not communion but intercommu-
> nion. There is no communion when two church-
> es expressly declare that they continue to remain
> independent entities. The Bonn Agreement is
> basically no more than a declaration of mutual
> recognition. It requires no change from the par-
> ties but respects the status quo of both commun-
> ions. In practice, especially in the eyes of other
> churches, they continue to live and witness as
> before.
>
> The first sentence of the Bonn Agreement illus-
> trates the difficulty very poignantly. It reads:
> "Each communion recognizes the catholicity and
> independence of the other and maintains its
> own." The positive meaning of the sentence is
> clear: each Church recognizes in the other the
> gift of catholicity and, while respecting the juris-
> dictional independence of the other Church,
> offers *communio in sacris* (sacramental sharing) in
> all respects. But the phrasing also reveals the hid-
> den contradiction: "and maintains its own
> catholicity." How can churches be catholic if they
> "maintain" their "own" catholicity? Is it not a
> contradiction in terms to speak of my "own"
> catholicity?[29]

Indeed, Vischer has a compelling point that cannot be glossed over because the local church's catholicity cannot be understood apart from its relationship with other local-universal churches throughout the world.

The dilemma set before us is a purely Western one. That is, our Christian identity in the Western church has become inherently divided through the various *confessional branches* of the church born out of the sixteenth-century Reformation. The Catholic Church in the West thus became divided after the sixteenth-century into the now two familiar general categories of Roman Catholic and Protestant/Reformed. Denominationalism has corrupted the very nature of the catholic and apostolic church of the ages because there is no longer an internal mutual interdependence and cooperation among these local churches. That is, the distinctive denominational/confessional differences, or what Zizioulas calls 'confessional pluralism,' on the local level does not exemplify the eucharistic character of the church as communion. Every denomination, whether Roman Catholic or Protestant/Reformed, struggles to transcend from its confessional/denominational identity and doctrine. But transcendence from these individualized identities on the local level is necessary if the church is to become a eucharistic communion once again. "Can we say that as the eucharist brings together Jew and Greek, male and female, black and white, it should also bring together Anglican and Lutheran and Orthodox, etc. in a certain local area?"[30] Zizioulas' question here alludes to the ecclesiastical conundrum found in the first clause of the 1931 Bonn Agreement.

A sharing in the sacraments with each other while maintaining a total independence on the local level is a superficial notion of communion and "denies catholici-ty."[31] *Intercommunion is not full communion* and it merely accommodates and perpetuates the division churches in the West are trying to overcome. Moreover, intercommunion is a weak relationship of mere acquaintance, whereas communion is based on a more intimated and co-operative relationship centered in love and freedom. The implied communion standard found in the 1931 Bonn Agreement moves beyond the mere "sharing of the sacraments" and compels both churches to seek common fellowship with each other united in the essentials of the Christian faith. This means change and transformation is inevitable for both churches. Communion always implies a certain transformation from *what was* to *what is* and *what will be*. If the 1931 Bonn Agreement is to be lived to its full potential, it means a death and a resurrection must occur for both churches. This is something fascinating yet also scary for most Anglicans and Old Catholics because change for some means a loss of past identity and allegiances.[32] Be not afraid! Jesus was still Jesus after the resurrection, but there was something different about him—he was changed for the better. So too with the church, we must all die to our relentless confessional/denominational allegiances that separate us, so to resurrect ourselves as the Catholic Church changed anew and united in our ancient doctrinal essentials for the betterment of all. Through this transformation of dying and rising we will be able to proclaim that the catholicity and unity of the church is found always on the local level, where each local-universal church independently co-operates with all other local-universal churches united in their diversity and love for each other. In the resurrected Catholic

Church "there is no 'mother or mistress of all churches.' Unity is achieved by mutual love and service, not by subjection to one centre."[33]

Conclusion

The *Bonn Agreement of 1931* is the most important ecumenical document of communion to date. It has the potential to bridge the confessional divisions that occurred in the Western church at the Reformation because it expresses communion in the essentials of faith found in early church doctrine, where much commonality and agreement among most mainline Christian churches is to be found with each other. The three principles of *doctrinal unity, mutual recognition, and independent cooperation* help to form the implicit eucharistic ecclesiology found in the 1931 Bonn Agreement. These three principles offer denominational churches in the West a dynamic paradigm of reunion in the essentials of the faith without having to sacrifice independent diversity on the local level. *The Bonn Agreement of 1931* is of crucial importance to both the study of Old Catholic eucharistic ecclesiology and its ongoing relationship with the Anglican Communion because it offers hope that one day the Catholic Church of the first five-centuries can be resurrected and transformed into a contemporary communion of diverse local-universal churches throughout the world confessing the name Christian with one voice.

CHAPTER FIVE: Conclusion

"Communion is not only an encounter between Christ and the individual believer (this aspect has shaped much of our eucharistic piety), but more importantly a community building event integrating each believer in the committed fellowship of brothers and sisters in Christ (cf. 1 Cor 11:29)"   —*Urs von Arx*[1]

THE OLD CATHOLIC MOVEMENT is a path that enriches the complex history of the universal church through the ages. The conciliar and sacramental nature of Old Catholicism is a gift to *remnant* Roman Catholics who feel estranged by their own church. Old Catholic eucharistic ecclesiology provides hope to those who want to live out their Catholicism in a healthy and meaningful manner in North America. My research has led me to the conclusion that the Old Catholic churches of the Union of Utrecht have provided a vision of the church's *being as communion* through the lens of the *ecclesia primitiva*, where the Catholic Church is fully manifested on the local level in the lived celebration of holy Eucharist.

Throughout this book I provided a perspective on the independent Old Catholic church groups in North America as they exist today, and contrasted it in varying ways to the Union of Utrecht's eucharistic ecclesiology of the local-universal church. I further asserted that the U.S. independent Old Catholic ecclesial groups *together* must boldly face that, to date, their movement is inherently disordered, fragmented, and spiritually suffers from the disease of clericalism to an extreme degree. Independent Old Catholics in North America *do not represent* the churches of the Union of Utrecht in any way, shape or form; independent Old Catholicism in North America is, by its very nature, a confusing oddity that has been perpetuated through the years by wandering bishops who have no local church. Granted, there are some independent Old Catholic bishops in the U.S. who do have semblances of a "local church" as defined by the Union of Utrecht and do good works of ministry in the name of our Triune God, however, these small churches are more the exception than the rule or normalcy in this regard.

Again, it is not my intention to be baselessly critical of the independent Old Catholic groups in North America— I am an independent Old Catholic priest living in the U.S.! As an ex-Roman Catholic, I find much solace and serenity in the Old Catholic faith, and the eucharistic ecclesiology of the Union of Utrecht has further provided me with a theological language to intelligently express my ideas of Catholicity apart from the dogmas and doctrines of Rome. In short, the conciliar and ecumenical ideas presented and ratified at Vatican II are being lived out in a most authentic manner by the Old Catholics of the Union of Utrecht. That is why I claim to be an Old Catholic, that is why most independents in the U.S. want to be Old Catholic, but we must realize that to do this means that we have to be comfortable living in the Diaspora of Old Catholicism in the U.S.—meaning, we are not in communion with the church we claim to be! In fact, we are not in communion with any historical and apostolic church; our very name claims our independency in this regard. This is a problem, and we must begin correcting it, we must begin cleaning the huge mess in our house. If Old Catholicism is to have any chance at establishing itself in the U.S., independent Old Catholic clergy and bishops need to first learn how to *surrender* their ego and self-aggrandizement at the door, *be totally honest* (not honest here and dishonest there) in admitting that as independent Old Catholics we are *powerless* and inherently disordered, *trust* that God will help us find our way, begin cleaning the house, and lastly *help others* to do the same. There is no question that there is a place for Old Catholicism in the U.S., but much in-house cleaning needs to be done beforehand, and we must be content in accepting that, like Moses, most of us will not see the promised land. After all, as Christians our serenity should lie in serving God and neighbor with our whole heart, without the burden of the end results—this is God's concern and not ours!

Lastly, in Chapter Four I assert that an ecclesiological convergence is occurring at this present time in history between the Anglicans and Old Catholics in ways never before seen. Here on the local level we can begin to observe a lived early church eucharistic ecclesiology surfacing in various dioceses in the Episcopal Church (USA).[2] The Episcopal Church is, beginning to resemble the Old Catholic Church, and the Old Catholic Church is beginning to resemble the Anglican Communion. In other words, what we are observing in contemporary history is the transformation of two local-universal church communions in the West, converging with each other ecclesiologically and sharing with each other the essential eucharistic character of communion and common mission in becoming the Catholic Church envisioned by early church theologians like St. Irenaeus, among others.

There is a place for "Vatican II" Catholics in the Old Catholic faith! There is a place where you can celebrate your sacramental life as a Catholic seeking unity in diversity in the Old Catholic faith! Independent Old Catholics need to realize that the eucharistic *charisma* of Old Catholicism is alive and well in the greater communion of the Episcopal Church, and in time we will need to find ways of fostering friendships with clergy and laity of the Episcopal Church. I firmly believe that no Old Catholic local church will ever exist in the U.S. without it being intimately related with the Episcopal Church (USA). We must remember that the Union of Utrecht and the Episcopal Church (USA) are in communion with each other, and endeavor to be one church! Hence, it is reasonable to conclude that Utrecht will never establish opposing dioceses in the U.S. against the Episcopal Church (USA). If we Old Catholics, living in the Diaspora of the U.S., truly want to be at home with our faith and be at peace with God and each other, then we must actively seek fellowship with the Episcopal Church (USA) on the local level any way we possibly can.

In short, Anglicans and Old Catholics are currently in the process of converging with one another ecclesiologically on the academic and local/practical levels of the church. The engagement that occurred over seventy years ago at Bonn between Anglicans and Old Catholics is coming to an end, and the marriage banquet of authentic communion centered in hospitality is getting closer at hand. All I can say is that I look forward to celebrating the honeymoon with you all one day!

APPENDIX A

THE DECLARATION OF THE
UNION OF UTRECHT (1889)

1. We adhere faithfully to the Rule of Faith laid down by St. Vincent of Lerins in these terms: *"Id teneamus, quod ubique, quod semper, quod ab omnibus creditum est; hoc est etenim vere proprieque catholicum."* For this reason we preserve in professing the faith of the primitive Church, as formulated in the œcumenical symbols and specified precisely by the unanimously accepted decisions of the Œcumenical Councils held in the undivided Church of the first thousand years.

2. We therefore reject the decrees of the so-called Council of the Vatican, which were promulgated July 18th, 1870, concerning the infallibility and the universal Episcopate of the Bishop of Rome, decrees which are in contradiction with the faith of the ancient Church, and which destroy

its ancient canonical constitution by attributing to the Pope the plentitude of ecclesiastical powers over all Dioceses and over all the faithful. By denial of this primatial jurisdiction we do not wish to deny the historical primacy which several Œcumenical Councils and Fathers of the ancient Church have attributed to the Bishop of Rome by recognizing him as the Primus inter pares.

3. We also reject the dogma of the Immaculate Conception promulgated by Pius IX in 1854 in defiance of the Holy Scriptures and in contradiction to the tradition of the centuries.

4. As for other Encyclicals published by the Bishops of Rome in recent times for example, the Bulls *Unigenitus* and *Auctorem fidei,* and the *Syllabus of 1864*, we reject them on all such points as are in contradiction with the doctrine of the primitive Church, and we do not recognize them as binding on the consciences of the faithful. We also renew the ancient protests of the Catholic Church of Holland against the errors of the Roman Curia, and against its attacks upon the rights of national Churches.

5. We refuse to accept the decrees of the Council of Trent in matters of discipline, and as for the dogmatic decisions of that Council we accept them only so far as they are in harmony with the teaching of the primitive Church.

6. Considering that the Holy Eucharist has always been the true central point of Catholic worship, we consider it our right to declare that we maintain with perfect fidelity the ancient Catholic doctrine concerning the Sacrament of

the Altar, by believing that we receive the Body and Blood
of our Saviour Jesus Christ under the species of bread and
wine. The Eucharistic celebration in the Church is neither
a continual repetition nor a renewal of the expiatory sacrifice which Jesus offered once for all upon the Cross: but
it is a sacrifice because it is the perpetual commemoration
of the sacrifice offered upon the Cross, and it is the act by
which we represent upon earth and appropriate to ourselves the one offering which Jesus Christ makes in
Heaven, according to the Epistle to the Hebrews 9:11-12,
for the salvation of redeemed humanity, by appearing for
us in the presence of God (Heb. 9:24). The character of
the Holy Eucharist being thus understood, it is, at the
same time, a sacrificial feast, by means of which the faithful in receiving the Body and Blood of our Saviour, enter
into communion with one another (I Cor. 10:17).

7. We hope that Catholic theologians, in maintaining the
faith of the undivided Church, will succeed in establishing an agreement upon questions which have been controverted ever since the divisions which arose between the
Churches. We exhort the priests under our jurisdiction to
teach, both by preaching and by the instruction of the
young, especially the essential Christian truths professed
by all the Christian confessions, to avoid, in discussing
controverted doctrines, any violation of truth or charity,
and in word and deed to set an example to the members.

8. By maintaining and professing faithfully the doctrine of
Jesus Christ, by refusing to admit those errors which by
the fault of men have crept into the Catholic Church, by
laying aside the abuses in ecclesiastical matters, together

with the worldly tendencies of the hierarchy, we believe that we shall be able to combat efficaciously the great evils of our day, which are unbelief and indifference in matters of religion.

Utrecht, 24th September 1889
   +Heykamp
   +Rinkel
   +Diependaal
   +Reinkens
   +Herzog

APPENDIX B

THE FOURTEEN THESES OF THE
OLD CATHOLIC UNION CONFERENCE
AT BONN—SEPTEMBER 14–16,1874

I. We agree that the apocryphal or deutero-canonical books of the Old Testament are not of the same canonicity as the books contained in the Hebrew Canon.

II. We agree that no translation of Holy Scripture can claim an authority superior to that of the original text.

III. We agree that the reading of Holy Scripture in the vulgar tongue cannot be lawfully forbidden.

IV. We agree that, in general, it is more fitting, and in accordance with the spirit of the Church, that the Liturgy should be in the tongue understood by the people.

V. We agree that Faith working by Love, not Faith without Love, is the means and condition of Man's justification before God.

VI. Salvation cannot be merited by "merit of condignity," because there is no proportion between the infinite worth of salvation promised by God and the finite worth of man's works.

VII. We agree that the doctrine of *"opera supererogationis"* and of a *"thesaurus meritorium sanctorum,"* i.e., that the overflowing merits of the Saints can be transferred to others, either by the rulers of the Church, or by the authors of the good works themselves, is untenable.

VIII. 1) We acknowledge that the number of sacraments was fixed at seven, first in the twelfth century, and then was received into the general teaching of the Church, not as a tradition coming down from the Apostles or from the earliest of times, but as the result of theological speculation.

2) Catholic theologians acknowledge, and we acknowledge with them, that Baptism and the Eucharist are *"principalia, praecipus, eximia salutis nostrae sacramenta."*

IX. 1) The Holy Scriptures being recognized as the primary rule of Faith, we agree that the genuine tradition, i.e. the unbroken transmission partly oral, partly in writing of the doctrine delivered by Christ and the Apostles is an authoritative source of teaching for all successive generations of Christians. This tradition is partly to be found in the consensus of the great ecclesiastical bodies standing in historical continuity with the primitive Church, partly to be gathered by scientific method from the written documents of all centuries.

2) We acknowledge that the Church of England; and the Churches derived through her, have maintained unbroken the Episcopal succession.

X. We reject the new Roman doctrine of the Immaculate Conception of the Blessed Virgin Mary, as being contrary to the tradition of the first thirteen centuries, according to which Christ alone is conceived without sin.

XI. We agree that the practice of confession of sins before the congregation or a Priest, together with the exercise of the power of the keys, has come down to us from the primitive Church, and that, purged from abuses and free from constraint, it should be preserved in the Church.

XII. We agree that "indulgences" can only refer to penalties actually imposed by the Church herself.

XIII. We acknowledge that the practice of the commemoration of the faithful departed, i.e. the calling down of a richer outpouring of Christ's grace upon them, has come down to us from the primitive Church, and is to be preserved in the Church.

XIV. 1) The Eucharistic celebration in the Church is not a continuous repetition or renewal of the propitiatory sacrifice offered once forever by Christ upon the cross; but its sacrificial character consists in this, that it is the permanent memorial of it, and a representation and presentation on earth of that one oblation of Christ for the salvation of redeemed mankind, which according to the Epistle to the Hebrews (9:11,12), is continuously presented in heaven by Christ, who now appears in the presence of God for us (9:24).

2) While this is the character of the Eucharist in reference to the sacrifice of Christ, it is also a sacred feast, wherein the faithful, receiving the Body and Blood of our Lord, have communion one with another (I Cor. 10:17).

APPENDIX C

THE 1931 BONN AGREEMENT[1]

Each communion recognizes the catholicity and independence of the other, and maintains its own.

Each communion agrees to admit members of the other communion to participate in the sacraments.

Intercommunion does not require from either communion the acceptance of all doctrinal opinion, sacramental devotion, or liturgical practice characteristic of the other, but implies that each believes the other to hold all the essentials of the Christian Faith.

Working Bibliography

Primary Sources

Athanasius. *On the Incarnation*, trans. by a Religious of C.S.M.V. and with an Introduction by C.S. Lewis. Crestwood, NY: St. Vladimir's Orthodox Theological Seminary, 1996.

Hippo, Augustine of. *On the Trinity Books 8-15*. Cambridge Texts in the History of Philosophy, ed. by Gareth B. Matthews and trans. by Stephen McKenna. Cambridge Press, 2002.

Lérins, Vincent of. *The Commonitory*. The Library of Christian Classics, "Early Medieval Theology," ed. and trans. by George E. McCracken, PhD, FAAR. Louisville ⟨London: Westminister John Knox Press, 2006.

.

Loyson, Père Hyacinthe. *Catholic Reform: Letters, Fragments, Discourses*, trans. by Madame Hyacinthe Loyson. London: Macmillan and Co., 1874.

Lyon, Irenaeus of. *Against Heresies, Book III*, in *The Christological Controversy*, ed. and trans. Richard A. Norris, Jr. Philadelphia, PA: Fortress Press, 1980.

Neale, J.M. *A History of the So-Called Jansenist Church of Holland*. John Henry and James Parker, 1858; reprint Berkeley, CA: Apocryphile Press ed., 2005.

Nyssa, Gregory of. *Concerning What We Should Think of Saying That There Are Not Three Gods to Ablabius*, in *The Trinitarian Controversy*, ed. and trans. William G. Rusch. Philadelphia: Fortress Press, 1980.

Secondary Sources

Afanassieff, Nicolas. *The Church Which Presides in Love* in John Meyendorff, ed. *The Primacy of Peter*. London: The Faith Press, 1963.

Avis, Paul. *The Identity of Anglicanism: Essentials of Anglican Ecclesiology*. London; NY: T&T Clark, 2007.

Baptism, Eucharist, and Ministry. World Council of Churches, Geneva, 1982.

Barnett, James Monroe. *The Diaconate: A Full and Equal Order*. Valley Forge, PA: Trinity Press International, 1995.

Berlis, Angela. *Episcopal—Synodical Church Structure: Some Reflections on Issues of Synodality and Authority from an Old Catholic Perspective,* in Rigney, James, ed. *Women as Bishops.* London; NY: Mowbray, 2008.

Buber, Martin. *I and Thou.* Walter Kaufman, trans. NY: Touchstone: Simon & Schuster, 1996.

Capetz, Paul E. *God: A Brief History.* Minneapolis, MN: Fortress Press, 2003.

Downey, Michael. *Altogether Gift: A Trinitarian Spirituality.* Maryknoll, NY: Orbis Books, 2000.

Gerrish, Brian A. *Grace and Gratitude: The Eucharistic Theology of John Calvin.* Minneapolis, MN: Fortress Press, 1993.

Giles, Richard. *Creating Uncommon Worship: Transforming the Liturgy of the Eucharist.* Collegeville, MN: Liturgical Press, 2004.

Huelin, Gordon, ed. *Old Catholics & Anglicans 1931-1981.* Oxford University Press, 1983.

Irwin, Kevin W. *Models of the Eucharist.* New York: Paulist Press, 2005.

Kavanagh, Aidan. *Elements of Rite: A Handbook of Liturgical* Style. New York: Pueblo Publishing Co., 1982

Kraft, Sigisbert. *Liturgical Renewal in the Old Catholic Church: Its Basis, Progress and Purpose*, in Best, Thomas F. and Heller, Dagmar, eds. *Worship Today: Understanding, Practice, Ecumenical Implications*. Geneva, WCC Publications 2004, Faith and Order Paper No. 194.

Leith, John H., ed. *Creeds of the Churches: A Reader in Christian Doctrine form the Bible to the Present*, 3rd ed. Louisville, KY: Westminister John Knox Press, 1982.

Macquarrie, John. *A Guide to the Sacraments*. New York, NY: The Continuum Publishing Co., 1997.

Melton, J. Gordon and Pruter, Karl. *The Old Catholic Sourcebook*. New York: Garland Publishing, 1983.

Moltmann, Jürgen. *The Trinity and the Kingdom: The Doctrine of God*. Minneapolis, MN: Fortress Press, 1993.

Moss, Claude B. *The Old Catholic Movement: Its Origins and History*, 2nd ed., rev. and enl. London: Society for Promoting Christian Knowledge, 1964; reprint Berkeley, CA: Apocryphile Press ed., 2005.

Nesmith, Michael, Rt. Rev. *The History and Beliefs of Old Catholicism and the Old Catholic Church of North America*. 2nd ed. Tampa, FL: St. Michael's Seminary, 2007.

Overy, Richard, ed. *Jansenism: Catholic Resistance to Authority from the Reformation to the French Revolution*. New York, NY: St. Martin's Press, Inc.

Pruter, Karl. *A History of the Old Catholic Church*. San Bernadino, CA: The Borgo Press, 1973.

Queen, André. *Old Catholic: History, Ministry, Faith & Mission*. New York, NY: iUniverse, Inc., 2003.

Radner, Ephraim and Turner, Philip. *The Fate of Communion: The Agony of Anglicanism and the Future of a Global Church*. Grand Rapids, Michigan: William B. Eerdmans Publishing Co.

Rudy, Kathy. *Sex and the Church: Gender, Homosexuality and the Transformation of Christian Ethics*. Boston, MA: Beacon Press, 1997.

The Harpercollins Encyclopedia of Catholicism, 1995 ed.

Tierney, Brian. *Foundations of the Conciliary Theory,* ed. Heiko Oberman, 2nd ed., enl. Cambridge University Press, 1995; reprint Leiden, New York, Köln: Brill, 1998.

Volf, Miroslav. *After our Likeness: The Church as the Image of the Trinity*. Grand Rapids, MI: Wm. B. Eerdmans Publishing Co.

Walker, Williston, et al. *A History of the Christian Church,* 4th ed. New York: Charles Scribner's Sons, 1985.

Zizioulas, John D. *Eucharist, Bishop, Church: The Unity of the Church in the Divine Eucharist and the Bishop during the First Three Centuries*, trans. Elizabeth Theokritoff. Brookline, MA: Holy Cross Orthodox Press 2001.

_____. *Being as Communion*. Crestwood, NY: St. Vladimir's Seminary Press, 1985.

_____. *Communion & Otherness*, ed. Paul McPartlan. New York, NY: T&T Clark, 2006.

Journal Articles

Aghiorgoussis, Bp. Maximos. "Theological and Historical Aspects of Conciliarity: Some Propositions for Discussion" in *Greek Orthodox Theological Review* 24, 1979.

Arx, Urs von, et al. "Towards Further Convergence: Anglican and Old Catholic Ecclesiologies." *Internationale Kirchliche Zietschrift* 96, 2006.

Hussey, M. Edmund. "Nicholas Afanassiev's Eucharistic Ecclesiology: A Roman Catholic Viewpoint," *Journal of Ecumenical Studies,* vol. 12, no. 2, 1975.

Maan, P.J. "The Meaning and Significance of Tradition According to the Old Catholic Conception" in *Ecumenical Review* 1.4, Summer 1949.

Plekon, Michael. "Always Everyone and Always Together: The Eucharistic Ecclesiology of Nicolas Afanasiev's *The Lord's Supper* Revisited," *St. Vladimir's Theological Quarterly* 41, no. 2-3, 1997.

Smit, Peter-Ben. "The Old Catholic View on Scripture and Tradition: A Short Study of a Theological Organism," in *Internationale Kirchliche Zeitschrift,* April-June 2007, Vol. 97.

Visser, Jan. *The Old Catholic Churches of the Union of Utrecht* in *International Journal for the Study of the Christian Church.* London: The Continuum Publishing Group Ltd., 2003.

Zscheile, Dwight. "A More True 'Domestic and Foreign Missionary Society': Toward a Missional Polity for the Episcopal Church," *Journal of Religious Leadership* 5, vol. 1 & 2, 2006.

Online Sources

Grace, Eden. "The Conciliar Nature of the Orthodox Church: Definition and Implications" [database on-line] (Quaker and Ecumenical Essays by Eden Grace, 2000, accessed 1 December 2007); available from http://www.edengrace. org/conciliar.html; Internet; accessed 5 February 2007.

Orzell, Laurence J. "Disunion of Utrecht: Old Catholics Fall Out over New Doctrines," *Touchstone: A Journal of Mere Christianity*, 2004 [magazine on-line]; available from http://www.touchstonemag.com/archives/article.php?id= 17-04-056-r; Internet; accessed 6 October 2007.

FOR FURTHER READING

Afanasiev, Nicholas. *The Church of the Holy Spirit*. Ed. by Michael Plekon and trans. by Vitaly Permiakov. Indiana: University of Notre Dame Press, 2007.

Burkhard, John J. *Apostolicity Then and Now: An Ecumenical Church in a Postmodern World*. Collegeville, MN: Liturgical Press, 2004.

Fox, Patricia A. *God as Communion: John Zizioulas, Elizabeth Johnson, and the Retrieval of the Symbol of the Triune God*. Collegeville, MN: Liturgical Press, 2001.

Johnson, Elizabeth A. *She Who Is: The Mystery of God in Feminist Theological Discourse*. New York, NY: The Crossroad Publishing Company, 1997.

Kelly, J.N.D. *Early Christian Doctrines*. London & New York: Continuum, 1958. Fifth, revised edition, New York: Continuum, 2006.

_____ *Early Christian Creeds*. London & New York: Continuum, 1950. Third edition, New York: Continuum, 2006.

Kempis, Thomas à. *The Imitation of Christ: A Modern Version of the Immortal Classic*. Image Books Edition, ed. by Harold C. Gardiner, S.J. Garden City, NY: Doubleday & Company, Inc., 1955.

Long, Edward LeRoy, JR. *Patterns of Polity: Varities of Church Governanence*. Cleveland, Ohio: The Pilgrim Press, 2001.

Lubac, Henry J. *Corpus Mysticum: The Eucharist and the Church in the Middle Ages*. Trans. by Gemma Simmonds, et al. Indiana: University of Notre Dame Press, 2006.

Nouwen, Henry J.M. *With Burning Hearts: A Meditation on the Eucharistic Life*. Maryknoll, NY: Orbis Books, 1994.

Shelley, Bruce L. *Church History in Plain Language*, updated 2nd ed. Nashville, TN: Thomas Nelson Publishers, 1995.

Wang, Lisa. *Sacramentum Unitatis Ecclesiasticae: The Eucharistic Ecclesiology of Henri de Lubac* in *Anglican Theological Review*, vol. 85, no. 1, Summer 2003.

Willis, David. *Clues to the Nicene Creed: A Brief Outline of the Faith*. Grand Rapids, MI/Cambridge, U.K.: William B. Eerdmans Publishing Company, 2005.

NOTES

Introduction

1   Throughout this text I use the term "Old Catholic" and/or "Old Catholic Church" to refer specifically to its canonical polity: the Union of Utrecht.

2   Claude B. Moss elaborates on this idea commenting: "The Old Catholic Movement is a revolt against the claims of the Papacy, but within Latin Christendom. Its position must be distinguished from that of the Eastern churches, which have never been either Latin or subject to the Papacy; from that of the Anglican churches, which were once both Latin and Papalist, but have ceased to be either, and have established in the English-speaking world a third form of Catholic Christianity, neither Latin or Eastern; and from that of Evangelical Christianity...which lays emphasis rather on the

personal experience of the individual than on his membership in the visible church. The Old Catholic Movement…is the heir of the anti-papal movements within Latin Christendom." Claude B. Moss, *The Old Catholic Movement: Its Origins and History*, 2nd ed., rev. and enl. (London: Society for Promoting Christian Knowledge, 1964; reprint Berkeley, CA: Apocryphile Press ed., 2005), 1.

3   See 'Appendix A,' *The Declaration of Utrecht, 1889*, para. 2, parenthesis added (English text)

4   The Old Catholic churches universally acknowledge the conciliar nature of the church, where the local *congregatio fidelium* (the whole assembly of the local faithful) possesses authority in the mission of the local- universal church, not just the bishop and the clergy.

5   Contemporary Old Catholic theology on the conciliar nature of the church has been largely influenced by the Orthodox Church's previously developed ecclesiology on the subject. For further reading on current Orthodox conciliarist thought, see: Eden Grace, *The conciliar nature of the Orthodox Church: definition and implications* [database on-line] (Quaker and Ecumenical Essays by Eden Grace, 2000, accessed 1 December 2007); available from http://www.edengrace.org/conciliar.html; Internet.

6   Bp. Maximos Aghiorgoussis, *Theological and historical aspects of conciliarity: some propositions for discussion* in *Greek Orthodox Theological Review* 24 (1979): 5.

7   Moss, 1.

8   Brian Tierney, *Foundations of the Conciliary Theory*, ed. Heiko Oberman, 2nd ed., enl. (Cambridge University Press, 1995; reprint Leiden, New York, Köln: Brill), 11.

9   *Ibid.*

10 Tierney argues that conciliar theory was not a novel secular political theory "thrust" upon the church from outside to try and solve the immediate contextual problem posed by the Great Schism of 1378; instead Tierney, among other church historians and ecclesiologists, believes the origins of the conciliar theory is embedded in the canons and theology of the Catholic Church. Further elaborated, "It is generally agreed that the theories of the Conciliarists themselves were not unprecedented novelties, invented at the end of the fourteenth century to solve the urgent problems of the Great Schism. Yet although the conciliar doctrines provide an important field of study for the political theorist as well as for the church historian, there has been no wholly adequate account of their origins and early development. [Franz] Bliemetzrieder...himself acknowledged that any really adequate investigation of their [conciliar] origins would necessitate an inquiry into the theological and canonistic traditions of the preceding centuries." *Foundations of the Conciliary Theory,* ed. Heiko Oberman, 2nd ed., enl. (Cambridge University Press, 1995; reprint Leiden, New York, Köln: Brill), 6, 12. (my italics).

11 Tierney, 16.

12   Williston Walker et al., *A History of the Christian Church,* 4th ed. (New York: Charles Scribner's Sons, 1985), 373-74.

13   Tierney, xiii

14   *Ibid.*

15   Tierney, xiv

16   Moss, 18.

17   *Ibid.*

18   Tierney, 6.

19   Moss, 18.

20   Frisians is now Western Germany. The city of Utrecht became Willibrord's archiepiscopal residence and the ecclesiastical capital of the Northern Netherlands.

21   Moss, 91.

22   J.M. Neale, *A History of the So-Called Jansenist Church of Holland* (John Henry and James Parker, 1858; reprint Berkeley, CA: Apocryphile Press ed., 2005), 63.

23   The dates represent the beginning and ending of this pope's pontifical reign.

24   Neale, 64.

25   Moss, 91.

26   The Great Schism had just broken out (1378) between Pope Urban VI (elected in Rome) and Pope Clement VII (elected at Fondi, France) all in the same year.

27   Neale, 78-79.

28   Willibrord was Archbishop of Frisones, and estab-
      lished his episcopal residency in Utrecht as has
      already been explicated above. The immediate suc-
      cessor of Willibrord (Boniface) was Archbishop of
      Mainz, and resided in Utrecht as well. The church
      of Utrecht, while remaining a simple bishopric until
      the sixteenth-century, was the direct lineage carrier
      of Willibrord and his successors because he was the
      founder (primate) of the local church of Holland.

29   Moss, 33.

30   Moss, 23.

31   cf. The Gallican Movement.

32   Walker, 666.

33   Walker 667. Semi-Pelagianism refers to teachings of
      a fifth-century theologian named Pelagius who
      taught that God's grace is found in the free-will and
      innate goodness of humanity.

34   The Harpercollins Encyclopedia of Catholicism, 1995
      ed., s.v. "Molina, Luis de."

35   The Harpercollins Encyclopedia of Catholicism, 1995
      ed., s.v. "Jesuits."

36   The Harpercollins Encyclopedia of Catholicism, 1995
      ed., s.v. "grace, actual."

37   Moss, 35.

38   Neale, 27.

39   Moss, 63.

40   Pasquier Quesnel (d. 1719) wrote and published a
      book entitled "Moral Reflexions on the New
      Testament" in 1671, which was later condemned in
      a papal Bull called *Unigenitus* as being Jansenist.
      101 heretical propositions were extracted from
      Quesnel's book and a new *Formulary* was drafted to
      recant these new so-called Jansenist teachings.
      Quesnel's book supplanted the original five propo-
      sitions of Jansen's *Augustinus* in determining who
      was or was not a "Jansenist." Interestingly, the
      Union of Utrecht's "Declaration of 1889" in its eight
      articles of faith and dogmatics (which every nation-
      al Old Catholic church must abide by) specifically
      rejects the papal document *Unigenitus* (1713) issued
      by Pope Clement XI condemning Quesnel's text, in
      addition to other papal decrees, as being contrary to
      the teachings of the ancient church *and* an instru-
      ment of attack on the rights of local churches.

41   A. Gazier, eminent early twentieth-century theolog-
      ical historian called the term *Jansenist*, "...a phan-
      tom invented by the Jesuits." William Doyle,
      *Jansenism: Catholic Resistance to Authority from the
      Reformation to the French Revolution*, ed. Richard
      Overy (New York, NY: St. Martin's Press, Inc.), 87.

42   Tradition has it that Cornelius Jansen studied and
      read all the works of Augustine twenty times over.
      He was an expert on the teachings of Augustine.

43   The "council" of Orange (526) was actually a small
      gathering of bishops who met for the consecration
      of a basilica in France. The small gathering of bish-
      ops was considered a council because Pope Felix III

(d. 530) supported the gathering by a papal letter
sent to the bishops proclaiming it as a local council
to discern and clarify Augustine of Hippo's teaching
on original sin, the need for grace, and double predestination. The local council's focus was to *clarify,
define,* and *interpret* Augustine's doctrine on grace
and free will in lieu of the controversial teachings of
Pelegianism and semi-Pelegianism in the local
Gallic (French) church. Meaning that, contextually
this council was convened to resolve a local church
(i.e. France) controversy on grace. Accordingly, the
council of Orange, "...affirmed that man's free will
has been so weakened by sin that he can of himself
neither believe in God nor love him. Grace is necessary for man's salvation...double predestination is
repudiated." Thus, the council of Orange authoritatively *clarified, defined,* and *interpreted* a more mod-
erate representation of Augustinianism for the
church, but in no way was this decree meant to be
the official doctrine on grace for the catholic (universal) church. The doctrine of grace has always
been an ambiguous teaching in the Roman church
because it never "dogmatized" (or decreed through
an ecumenical council) this teaching of Augustine's.
Traditionally, however, Augustine's work on the
teaching of grace has been primarily taught (though
not fully embraced, as is seen in the council of
Orange) and revered in the Roman church in addition to most major Western Church denominations.
*Creeds of the Churches: A Reader in Christian Doctrine
form the Bible to the Present*, ed. John H. Leith, 3rd
ed. (Louisville, KY: Westminister John Knox Press,
1982), 37.

44   Various contemporary church historians, like J. McManners (1998), state that "one thing we cannot do is to define 'jansenism;'" furthermore "what they [those individuals and groups labeled Jansenist] had in common was not so much content as a tendency. Jansenism meant resistance to living (papal) authority in the Catholic Church." Doyle, 86-87.

45   See Moss, p. 335 (middle of first full paragraph).

46   P.J. Maan, *The Meaning and Significance of Tradition according to the Old Catholic conception* in *Ecumenical Review* 1.4 (Summer 1949): 4.

47   There is ecumenical precedence to make such a claim because of the semi-successful ecumenical 1982 Lima text entitled *Baptism, Eucharist, and Ministry.*

48   Paul E. Capetz, *God: A Brief History* (Minneapolis, MN: Fortress Press, 2003), 172.

CHAPTER TWO

1   John 17:11 NRSV (New Revised Standard Version).

2   Mattijs Ploeger, *Catholicity, Apostolicity, the Trinity and the Eucharist in Old Catholic Ecclesiology,* in *Towards Further Convergence: Anglican and Old Catholic Ecclesiologies,* ed. Urs von Arx, et al., *Internationale Kirchliche Zietschrift* 96 (2006): 19.

3   I believe that the eucharistic nature of the church goes beyond its sacramental character, permeating the entire theology and essence of the church because it expresses the grace and gratitude of the

baptized to God the Father for giving them a share in Christ's *ontological* personhood in the power of the Holy Spirit. See John Zizioulas, *Being as Communion* (Crestwood, NY: St. Vladimir's Seminary Press, 1985), especially pp. 23-24.

4   Clergy is meant here to include priests as well as deacons.

5   Ploeger, 17.

6   Although Anglicans and Old Catholics share a very close understanding of eucharistic ecclesiology, there is still an internal "lack of agreed definitions in respect of much of [Anglican] ecclesiology (Podmore, 46),"especially between the local (national) level and the Communion level in Anglicanism. This is not so with the Union of Utrecht in that there is a common theological and ecclesiological understanding between the autonomous national churches of the Union of Utrecht and its conference of national bishops (a/k/a the IBC). The Union of Utrecht's eucharistic ecclesiology is slightly different from that of the more "modest" Anglican ecclesiology in how it understands and approaches the concept of shared authority between that of the local national church-es and its Conference of Bishops. I will elaborate in greater detail on this topic in section three of this chapter. For further reading concerning Anglican eucharistic ecclesiology and the Anglican Communion's understanding of ecclesial authority, see Colin Podmore, *Collegiality, Conciliarity and Primacy: An Anglican Perspective*, in *Towards Further*

Convergence: Anglican and Old Catholic Ecclesiologies, ed. Urs von Arx, et al., *Internationale Kirchliche Zietschrift* 96 (2006), especially pp. 46-49; Ephraim Radner and Philip Turner, *The Fate of Communion: The Agony of Anglicanism and the Future of a Global Church* (Grand Rapids, Michigan: William B. Eerdmans Publishing Co.), especially pp. 90-94; and Paul Avis, *The Identity of Anglicanism: Essentials of Anglican Ecclesiology* (NY, London: T&T Clark, 2007), esp. pp. 81-108.

7   Marinus Kok, *Constitutions of the Old Catholic Churches in Old Catholics & Anglicans 1931-1981,* ed. Gordon Huelin (Oxford University Press, 1983), 17.

8   *Ibid.*

9   Zizioulas, *Being as Communion,* 190.

10   I state here that the early church of the first ten-centuries was *ideally* unified in the faith because history has shown that there has yet to be a time when full concord and peace permeated the body of Christ on earth. All one has to do is read Paul's epistle to the Galations in the New Testament to understand my point here. Having stated this, I do believe that the organic and dynamic nature of the one, holy, catholic, and apostolic church has conciliarly been made manifest in the ecumenical church councils of the first ten-centuries because its teachings have been (for the most part) *received* by the universal church (east and west) through the ages up to today as being orthodox (correct) and constitutive to the work of the Holy Spirit. Hence, the

ancient *conciliar* nature of the church, exemplified in the above early church councils, dismisses any notion of sole constituted power or unity centered in the Roman church's magisterial *infallible* institution or in any other ecclesial institution for that matter.

11   Kok, 18.

12   This section will not focus in great detail on the controversy surrounding the *theological* doctrine of the pope's infallibility decreed at Vatican I. Although the infallibility doctrine of Vatican I is a vital and worthwhile research topic to ponder, it goes beyond our current study and cannot be properly explicated in the limited space provided here. We will, however, focus briefly on this historical event because it cannot be completely ignored or glossed over due to the profound effect it had on the *birthing* of the Union of Utrecht and its later formative eucharistic ecclesiology.

13   Kok. 18.

14   *Ibid.*

15   Fr. Hyacinthe is mentioned in Moss' book *The Old Catholic Movement* (see pp. 199, 251-52, 283-84, 325, 332) as a priest who was against the infallibility doctrine being promulgated at the Vatican I council. Other than this brief mentioning of Loyson in Moss' text one could easily pass over and forget this eloquent orator and writer in the chronicles of history, if not for the resurgence of Fr. Hyacinthe's book published in 1874 entitled *Catholic Reform:*

Letters, Fragments, Discourses. This book is very difficult to obtain because of its outdatedness. It is,
however, one of the most important books that I
have read because it brings the Old Catholic movement and the Vatican I controversy alive in ways no
history book like Moss' could ever do! It is my hope
that this book gets put back into print circulation
because many will find Fr. Hyacinthe's words to be
eloquent, heartfelt, and very prophetic for his day.
According to Hyacinthe, "Men pass away, and their
works with them; but the truth of the Lord abideth
for ever"! Thanks be to God that the work of this
great priest has not been completely lost to the
church. Fr. Père Hyacinthe Loyson, *Catholic Reform:
Letters, Fragments, Discourses,* trans. Madame
Hyacinthe Loyson (London: Macmillan and Co.,
1874), 62.

16   *Ibid.*

17   See Karl Pruter and J. Gordon Melton, *The Old
Catholic Sourcebook* (New York: Garland Publishing,
1983), p. 11; and Karl Pruter, *A History of the Old
Catholic Church* (San Bernadino, CA: The Borgo
Press, 1973), esp. p. 14.

18   Loyson, 62.

19   Moss refers to this conference as "...the first of a
long series of Old Catholic congresses," and that
there were "300 Old Catholic sympathizers present." Moss is correct about the occurrence of this
conference, but contemporary Old Catholic historians stress that at the time this conference occurred
the term "old Catholic" was just being coined and

theologians like Döllinger (albeit excommunicated from the Roman church by this time) still thought of themselves as remaining faithful to the Roman Catholic Church. In other words, the idea of "Old Catholic" being a completely separate polity was just at its conception stage, and it is highly questionable whether these theologians considered themselves to be a completely separate denomination from that of the Roman Catholic communion they so cherished. The three hundred "others" that attended this conference were not so much supporters of Old Catholicism the polity, but sympathizers with the position that this group of old Catholic theologians took against the Vatican I council. Moss' words can be misleading in his text (if not read carefully) when he indirectly alludes to the idea that these theologians understood the term "Old Catholic" to mean a separate polity from that of the Roman Catholic Church. Further stated, Old Catholicism, as we understand the polity today, was just beginning to be conceived during this time in history and was a very fragile idea at best. See Moss, p. 234.

20   *The Harpercollins Encyclopedia of Catholicism,* 1995 ed., s.v. "Ecumenical Councils."

21   Döllinger further remarks about his excommunication from Rome in a declaration stating that "…we find for the first time (history shows no other example of it in the course of eighteen centuries) that excommunication is thundered against men, not for maintaining and propagating a new doctrine, but for seeking to preserve the old faith as they received

it from their parents and teachers in school and Church, and for not being willing to receive a different doctrine, nor to change their faith as they change their garments." Loyson, 69.

22   Loyson, 64.

23   Loyson, 136. Loyson's footnote for the above quote identifies the "learned Catholic of Germany" mentioned in the above quote as Professor Maassen, and the quote was taken from a speech Maassen gave before the University of Vienna (1871), p. 136 (footnote 1).

24   Moss, 236.

25   Jan Visser, *The Old Catholic Churches of the Union of Utrecht* in *International Journal for the Study of the Christian Church* (London: The Continuum Publishing Group Ltd., 2003), my italics, 73. This quote by Visser needs to be clearly understood and not ignored. Although we will thoroughly study the so-called Old Catholic jurisdictions in North America in chapter three, I am compelled to quote Visser's footnote to the above quote when he states, "In the USA there are small communities directed by *episcope vagantes* (independent 'wandering' bishops), self-styled with or without the addition of the title 'Old Catholic'. They do not belong to the Union of Utrecht and in using the title 'Old Catholic' they cause confusion, as was recently the case when one of them, described as 'Old Catholic', ordained several Roman Catholic women as priests on a ship on the Danube." Visser, 73 (footnote 3).

26   Günter Esser, *Episcopacy—Conciliarity—Collegiality —Primacy: The Theology and the Task of Episcopacy from an Old Catholic Perspective,* in *Towards Further Convergence: Anglican and Old Catholic Ecclesiologies,* ed. Urs von Arx, et al., *Internationale Kirchliche Zietschrift* 96 (2006): 74.

27   For further reading on the subject of Old Catholic church synodality see Angela Berlis' essay in *Woman as Bishops,* ed. James Rigney with Mark D. Chapman (NY, London: Mowbray, 2008), esp. pp. 62-71.

28   Moss, v.

29   Moss, 21.

30   Current Old Catholic ecclesiology is rapidly moving beyond these politico-national theories of the four-teenth and nineteenth-centuries, and has adopted a more Orthodox trinitarian and eucharistic under-standing of the Church's nature.

31   Jan Visser, *Old Catholic Spirituality,* in *Old Catholics & Anglicans 1931-1981,* ed. Gordon Huelin (Oxford University Press, 1983), 98.

32   Kok, 10.

33   Of course the "norm" in understanding the theolog-ical "essentials" is limited to the theological doc-trines of the councils of the first ten-centuries for Old Catholics. This understanding obviously con-stricts the theological understanding of "unity in diversity" in a way that some would not agree with.

34   Zizioulas, *Being as Communion,* 135.

35   Kok, 22.

36   Visser, *The Old Catholic Churches of the Union of Utrecht* in *International Journal for the Study of the Christian Church* (London: The Continuum Publishing Group Ltd., 2003), 75.

37   Ploeger, 9.

38   Ploeger, 9-10.

39   *Ibid.*

40   Mark 8:27 NRSV (New Revised Standard Version).

41   Ploeger, 19-20.

42   As a "eucharistic fellowship" the local church is not an isolated entity nor is it merely *part* of a universal whole, but is in fact local and universal at the same time. Every local church is at the same time the local *catholic* (universal) church through its eucharistic communion with other local-universal churches. In other words, according to Zizioulas and other eucharistic ecclesiologists, the communion of the local eucharistic community *naturally* transcends what is local to the universal level and vice versa. Accordingly, "what each eucharistic community, therefore, was meant to reveal, was not part of Christ but the whole of Christ and not a partial or local unity but the full eschatological unity of all in Christ." Russian Orthodox eucharistic ecclesiologist, Nicholas Afanasiev, further attests to this local-universal paradoxical nature of the church stating, "it [the local church] could not shut itself in or refuse to be acquainted with happenings in other churches: for anything that happened in other [local] churches, as well as its own, happened in the

Church of God, the one and only church...Every local church must be in concord with all the other churches...This means, empirically speaking, that every local church accepts and makes its own anything that happens in each fellow-church." Zizioulas, *Being as Communion*, 154; Nicolas Afanasiev, *The Church which Presides in Love,* in Michael Plekon, "Always Everyone and Always Together: The Eucharistic Ecclesiology of Nicolas Afanasiev's *The Lord's Supper* Revisited," *St. Vladimir's Theological Quarterly* 41, no. 2-3 (1997): 154.

43   1 Corinthians 1:23 NRSV (New Revised Standard Version).

44   John D. Zizioulas, *Communion & Otherness,* ed. Paul McPartlan (New York, NY: T&T Clark), 261.

45   *Ibid.*, 157.

46   Cf. Athanasius' theological work "On the Incarnation" provides a good example of the original use of the Greek word *hypostasis* as being synonymous with words like *image, substance* or *essence.* Athanasius, *On the Incarnation,* trans. by a Religious of C.S.M.V. and with an Introduction by C.S. Lewis (Crestwood, NY: St. Vladimir's Orthodox Theological Seminary, 1996), especially pp. 40-47.

47   Zizioulas, *Being as Communion*, 17.

48   Zizioulas, *Communion & Otherness*, 158.

49   *Ibid.*, 56.

50   *Ibid.*, 159.

51 For a more detailed study on this subject of human personhood see Zizioulas' *Communion & Otherness,* especially pp. 55-57.

52 *Ibid.,* 159.

53 Jürgen Moltmann, *The Trinity and the Kingdom* (Minneapolis, MN: Fortress Press, 1993), 175.

54 *Ibid.*

55 Zizioulas, *Communion & Otherness,* 118.

56 *Ibid.,* 115.

57 *Ibid.*

58 Moltmann, 175.

59 Cf. John D. Zizioulas, *Being as Communion,* pp. 40-44.

60 Zizioulas, *Communion & Otherness,* 116.

61 Zizioulas, *Being as Communion.,* 41.

62 Zizioulas, *Communion & Otherness,* 119.

63 Gregory of Nyssa, *Concerning What We Should Think of Saying That There Are Not Three Gods to Ablabius,* in *The Trinitarian Controversy,* ed. and trans. William G. Rusch (Philadelphia: Fortress Press, 1980), 155.

64 Zizioulas, *Being as Communion,* 106.

65 *Ibid.,* 107-08.

66 *Id.,* 107.

67 See Zizioulas, *Communion and Otherness,* pp. 237-243, esp. p. 238.

68   Miroslav Volf, *After our Likeness: The Church as the Image of the Trinity* (Grand Rapids, MI: Wm. B. Eerdmans Publishing Co.), 84.

69   *Ibid.*

70   Zizioulas, *Communion & Otherness*, 261.

71   Zizioulas, *Being as Communion*, 110.

72   It begs the question here as to what humanity's true nature is. Another words, human nature ceases to be viewed ontologically (ground of *being*) and becomes an individualized moral and psychological phenomena. It's the idea that stresses Christ's individual humanity and nature, and is associated with a rational, existential humanism of the conscious self. Thus communion and ontology is obliterated by the false sense of humanity's individual understanding of the *self* in this regard.

73   *Ibid.*, 110-11.

74   I have been heavily influenced by this pneumatologically constituted christology as taught by John Zizioulas. It should also be noted here that Old Catholic Christology and ecclesiology has been influenced by this theology because it stresses the importance of relationship as being the essence of humanity's image and likeness of God's being as Trinity. For further reading on this subject please see Zizioulas, *Being as Communion*, especially pp. 110–114.

75   Zizioulas, *Being as Communion*, 130.

76   *Id.,* 132.

77   *Id.,* 111-12.

78   *Ibid.*

79   Gregory of Nyssa, 157. Note also that early church Father Irenaeus of Lyon asserts this understanding of Christ and the Holy Spirit against 'individualizing' Christ's personhood when he states, "By the name 'Christ' is connoted one who anoints, the one who is anointed, and the ointment itself with which he is anointed. Now, in point of fact, the Father has anointed, but the Son has been anointed—in the Spirit who is the ointment. That is why the Logos says through Isaiah, 'The Spirit of God is upon me because he has anointed me' (Isa. 61:1), referring at once to the anointing Father, the anointed Son, and the ointment, which is the Spirit." Irenaeus of Lyon, *Against Heresies, Book III,* in *The Christological Controversy,* ed. and trans. Richard A. Norris, Jr. (Philadelphia, PA: Fortress Press), 51.

80   Zizioulas, *Communion & Otherness,* 261.

81   This synthesizing of Christ and the Spirit in ecclesiology is also inherently and historically Old Catholic. The 1871 Munich conference discourse entitled *The Ancient Primacy and the Modern Papacy* promulgated this same theological thought in stating, "The unity of the Church is, then, *primarily* an inward unity, of which the Holy Spirit is the author," Loyson, 137 (my italics).

82   Ploeger, 19.

83   John Macquarrie, *A Guide to the Sacraments*, (New York, NY: The Continuum Publishing Co., 1997), 37.

84   Brian A. Gerrish, *Grace and Gratitude: The Eucharistic Theology of John Calvin* (Minneapolis, MN: Fortress Press, 1993), vii.

85   Zizioulas, *Being as Communion*, 111 (my italics on "personal").

86   See Ploeger, p. 19.

87   Zizioulas, *Being as Communion*, 143.

88   Sarah Aebersold, *The Church Local and Universal* in *Towards Further Convergence: Anglican and Old Catholic Ecclesiologies,* ed. Urs von Arx, et al., *Internationale Kirchliche Zietschrift* 96 (2006): (my italics) 86.

89   See Ploeger, especially pp. 10-11.

90   I am *only* referring here to those bishops in the U.S. who *specifically* claim and identify themselves to be part of the Independent (Old) Catholic movement/tradition.

91   Aebersold, (my italics) 89; See also Zizioulas, *Being as Communion*, pp. 238-240. I am aware that this definition of the local church may be perceived as being too traditionalist, and seems to abandon ecumenical dialogue with non-episcopal Western Christian denominations. Old Catholic theologian, Urs von Arx, addresses this issue in one of his essays in the *Internationale Kirchliche Zeitschrift* (Union of Utrecht's official theological journal) stat-

ing, "But it is here where Old Catholic mainstream ecclesiology would often be more traditional and thus unable to acknowledge a (non-episcopal) church, with which to live in visible unity is not (yet) possible, as a 'true' church, or reluctant in placing mutual eucharistic sharing as the *first* stage in a process of growing together into full ecclesial communion, ministerial sharing coming *later* [what I deem a reversal of the implied theological hierarchy and spiritual values and a form of latent clericalisation]." One must also take into account that Old Catholic theology intentionally seeks out ecumenical relations with other local churches not of its tradition, e.g. the Anglican Communion. This theology is, however, limiting because of how it defines "local church." Interestingly the Lima text of 1982, published by the World Council of Churches, acknowledges this theological conundrum by stressing that churches who do not have episcopal succession may need to regain it in as much as churches who possess apostolic succession must broaden its ideas about episcopal succession allowing for diversity and difference to enter the church as something positive and life-giving. – Urs von Arx, *Unity and Communion, Mystical and Visible*, in *Towards Further Convergence: Anglican and Old Catholic Ecclesiologies,* ed. Urs von Arx, et al., *Internationale Kirchliche Zietschrift* 96 (2006): 161.

92   Biblical theologian, Marilyn Salmon, emphasizes in her book *ad infinitum* that the early Jesus believing communities founded by Paul were not yet separated from Judaism, but rather were considered a

small diverse sect within Judaism having no real central authority governance wise. See Marilyn Salmon, *Preaching Without Contempt: Overcoming Anti-Judaism* (Minneapolis, MN: Fortress Press, 2006), esp. p. 27 (top paragraph).

93   See First Corinthians 16:19-20, and Romans 16:16.

94   See Esser, p. 72.

95   Esser, (my italics) 73.

96   Ploeger, 12.

97   See Zizioulas, *Being as Communion*, p. 145.

98   Visser, *The Old Catholic Churches of the Union of Utrecht*, 78.

99   Ploeger, 20.

100   Michael Downey, in his book *Altogether Gift: A Trinitarian Spirituality*, uses the metaphor of Gift, Given, and Gifting to describe the economic activity of the Trinity. I like this metaphoric way of describing the Trinity because grace is embodied as *Gift* toward the 'other' in the Triune persons. The Father is the Gift, and the Son is Given, but I do not agree with Downey's description of the Holy Spirit as "Gifting" because it implies that the spirit is an ancillary to the Father and Son, whereas I prefer the term "Gifted" because it better describes the activity of the Spirit as the "Able One" that eternally establishes (in freedom and love) the will of the Father in Christ Jesus – See Michael Downey, *Altogether Gift: A Trinitarian Spirituality*, (Maryknoll, NY: Orbis Books, 2000), pp. 42-44, esp. chapter

two: "A Grammer of Gift," section "Giver, Given, Gifting" at pp. 55-59.

101 Eph. 5:29-33 NRSV (New Revised Standard Version).

102 Having stated this, there still seems to be a sense of hesitation with the theologians of the Union of Utrecht about whether or not to outright reject the doctrine of transubstantiation. I mentioned above that transubstantiation was declared a *dogma* (a binding truth of the faith) at the council of Trent; however, it was also previously declared as an official teaching of the church at the Fourth Lateran council (1215) – a council not explicitly rejected or embraced by the Old Catholics. Suffice it to state here that Old Catholicism views transubstantiation as a philosophical method of trying to explain what is ultimate mystery, and should not be binding on the faithful as a *dogma* (qualified Truth) of the church because it is not in harmony with the teachings of the early church, nor is its definition theological in essence. Further stated, Swiss Old Catholic Bishop and theologian Urs Küry, while in ecumenical dialogue with the Anglican Communion, "...urged that the *fact* of Christ's real presence is what matters (the 'Dass') while the *manner* or *how* (the 'Wie') must be left open." J. Robert Wright, *Anglican and Old Catholic Theology Compared* in *Old Catholics & Anglicans 1931-1981* ed. Gordon Huelin (Oxford University Press, 1983), 134. See also Moss, pp. 333-34.

103 Gerrish, 73.

104 See Ploeger, p. 20.

105 Zizioulas, *Being as Communion,* 133.

106 Ploeger, 20-21.

107 See Zizioulas, *Being as Communion,* pp. 229-234, especially p. 234.

108 Zizioulas, *Being as Communion,* 163.

109 Zizioulas, *Being as Communion,* 165-66.

110 Esser, 76.

111 Kevin W. Irwin, *Models of the Eucharist* (New York: Paulist Press, 2005), 218-19.

112 Visser, 76.

113 I concur with Irwin in that the Eucharist is a sacrifice (an offering to God) that is sacramental (mystery experienced through sacred signs and symbols) in nature to perpetuate (and re-member) Christ's one and only death on the cross, as well as being a sacred meal that the local church receives in communion with one another for sustenance and strength in the mission of spreading the good news. For further reading about Catholic models of the Eucharist please see Kevin W. Irwin, *Models of the Eucharist* (New York: Paulist Press, 2005), esp. pp. 218-19.

114 Visser, 77.

115 *Ibid.*

116 *Ibid.*

117 Ploeger, 23.

118   Visser, 79.

119   See Sigisbert Kraft, *The Hymnology of the Old Catholic Church as a Reflection of its Self-Comprehension* (in Appendix III of book) in *Old Catholics & Anglicans: 1931-1981*, pp. 168-170, esp. p. 170 (third full paragraph).

120   Some theologians differentiate between the big 'T' and the little 't' when referring to tradition. I make no etymological distinction in this regard. Tradition is tradition in as much as Catholic is catholic. The meanings that are attached to these words are both-and in my opinion, to which I assert that there is no difference between capitalizing and not capitalizing the first letters when it comes to defining these words.

121   P.J. Mann, *The Meaning and Significance of Tradition: according to the Old Catholic conception,* in *The Ecumenical Review* (Summer 1949, Vol. 1.4), 393.

122   *Ibid.*

123   A very insightful essay was recently written in the Union of Utrecht's theological journal (the *IKZ*) by Peter-Ben Smit regarding the organic relationship between scripture and tradition. Specifically, Smit studies the late Archbishop Andreas Rinkel's dynamic and ecumenically driven theological tome on this subject and its ecumenical dialectic with the Orthodox and Anglican churches. Smit's essay continues the important dialogue, both within and outside, the Old Catholic Church about the relationship between tradition and scripture: Peter-Ben

Smit, *The Old Catholic View on Scripture and Tradition: A Short Study of a Theological Organism*, in *Internationale Kirchliche Zeitschrift* (April-June 2007, Vol. 97), 106-123.

124 Mann, 395.

125 *Id.*, 396.

126 *Id.*, 397.

127 See Ploeger p. 25, especially pp. 15-16.

128 Zizioulas, *Being as Communion*, 174.

129 Ploeger, 16; See also Zizioulas, *Being as Communion*, especially, p. 177.

130 Kok, 19-20.

131 Visser, (my italics) 77.

132 Esser, 77.

133 *Id.*, 88-89.

134 Visser, 79.

135 Wright, 134.

136 Kathy Rudy, *Sex and the Church: Gender, Homosexuality and the Transformation of Christian Ethics*, (Boston, MA: Beacon Press, 1997), 97.

137 See also Sigisbert Kraft, *Liturgical Renewal in the Old Catholic Church: Its Basis, Progress and Purpose*, in *Worship Today: Understanding, Practice, Ecumenical Implications* (Thomas F. Best and Dagmar Heller, eds., Geneva, WCC Publications 2004, Faith and Order Paper No. 194), esp. p. 135.

138 Plekon, 166.

139 Plekon, 168.

140 See Kraft, pp. 130-131.

141 See Kraft, pp. 131 and 137 (last paragraph).

142 It should be clearly stated that contextually and historically the church of the moment is wholly different from that of the early church of the first ten-centuries, and I am not suggesting that the classical and contemporary Old Catholic theologians naively claim or want to revert the church *wholly* back to that time in history. First, it's impossible to do such a thing because socially and contextually the church of our day is different from the early church in many ways; it is, however, possible to rediscover the ancient church fathers' teachings from the second and third centuries on up (as well as St. Paul's "Jesus the Messiah" believing house communities in New Testament scripture), re-establishing and integrating, as best as possible, these teachings and styles of worship within the church of today. This, I believe, is exactly what the classical and contemporary Old Catholic theologians have in mind and continue to stress in their writings when referring to the theology and liturgy of the early church.

143 Kraft, 131.

144 Richard Giles, *Creating Uncommon Worship: transforming the liturgy of the Eucharist* (Collegeville, MN: Liturgical Press, 2004), 67.

145 This holistic reality of the eucharistic liturgy is found in the liturgical actions and prayers of the

presiding minister and the gathered assembly throughout the service. Meaning, the Christian triune God is experienced in many and various ways in the liturgical celebration through touching, kissing, smell, taste, sight, and as well as through the spoken words of prayer, scripture and the gospel text. Overall, there is a real and tangible sense of the holy in the Old Catholic eucharistic liturgy. For a more thorough and well articulated *liturgical* understanding of eucharistic ecclesiology, see Richard Giles' book "Creating Uncommon Worship: transforming the liturgy of the Eucharist."

146   Kraft, 135.

147   Kraft, 137.

CHAPTER THREE

1   The terms 'North America' and 'United States' are used interchangeably throughout this essay. Obviously this puts limits on the meaning of the word 'North America'; however, this is inevitable considering that the author is socially and contextually constrained to the current Old Catholic dilemma in the United States of America and not elsewhere (e.g. British Columbia, Canada, etc.) within the continental North America.

2   This statement will become clearer as the reader continues to read each of the sections of this chapter.

3   Specifically, this refers to the classical, yet still currently embraced, 'Pruterian' school of thought

promulgated by the well known American 'Old Catholic' self-published author Bishop Karl Pruter.

4   Pruter, *The Old Catholic Sourcebook*, 3.

5   Many American independent Old Catholic clergy (i.e., Pruter) do not regard the Union of Utrecht as the defining ecclesiastical body for Old Catholicism in the world. They concur with Pruter in this regard and believe that the Union of Utrecht is not the defining source for the term "Old Catholic," and is at best a narrow definition of the term. See Pruter and Melton, *The Old Catholic Sourcebook*, first paragraph, p. 3.

6   Martin Buber, *I and Thou,* trans. Charles Scibner's Sons (NY: First Touchstone Edition, 1996), esp. pp. 53-85.

7   For an excellent review of how this ecclesiological system evolved see Nicholas Afanassieff's essay, "The Church Which Presides in Love," in *The Primacy of Peter,* ed. John Meyendorff (London: The Faith Press, 1963), esp. pp. 57-73.

8   In his books, Pruter (as well as his contemporaries) focus' mostly on the history of Old Catholicism. This is a telling insight because by focusing almost solely on the history of the Old Catholic Church, the reader can easily infer from these independent groups that a) the Old Catholic movement's importance was in its historical and canonical fight against papal supremacy (a dilemma concerned more about discipline than about theology), thus b) giving the impression that there is little theological

difference between Roman Catholicism and Old Catholicism to date. See Pruter, *History of the Old Catholic Church* (San Bernardino, CA: The Borgo Press, 1973)

9   See Karl Pruter, *History of the Old Catholic Church*, esp. pp. 12-15, and pp. 24-28; see also the last three paragraphs on p. 66.

10   See Alexander Schmemann's essay, "The Idea of Primacy in Orthodox Ecclesiology," in *The Primacy of Peter*, esp. p. 35.

11   See self-published American author Andre' Queen, *Old Catholic: History, Ministry, Faith & Mission* (New York, NY: iUniverse, Inc., 2003), pp. xi-1; esp. pp. 12-14; and Rt. Rev. Michael NeSmith, *The History and Beliefs of Old Catholicism and the Old Catholic Church of North America,* 2nd ed. (Tampa, FL: St. Michael's Seminary, 2007), esp. p. 26 (introduction).

12   See Queen, *Old Catholic: History, Ministry, Faith & Mission*, esp. Chapter 2 entitled *The Old Catholic Churches in the Americas*, pp. 20-29; and Pruter, *History of the Old Catholic Church*, pp. 65-66.

13   See Moss, esp. p. 308 (middle of first full paragraph); Jan Visser, *The Old Catholic Churches of the Union of Utrecht*, esp. p. 73.

14   See, Moss, p. 291 (middle paragraph).

15   Moss, 291.

16   Moss, 290.

17   See, Queen, p. 2.

18   Queen, 22.

19   *Ibid.*

20   Moss' book *The Old Catholic Movement* has proven itself through the test of time to be *the* most accurate Old Catholic historical book written in English, and is respected by both Union of Utrecht and Anglican theologians to date. Dr. Moss was part of the still existent St. Willibrord Society of Anglican and Old Catholic theologians, and he emerged in the 1950's as '…an authority on the Old Catholic Churches, gradually gaining the respect and trust of the Old Catholic bishops (of the Union of Utrecht)…' John Burley, *The Society of St. Willibrord: (a) Its History* in *Old Catholics & Anglicans 1931-1981*, 67. Interestingly, Queen's ideas presented above are remarkably similar to Pruter's when he states, 'he [Vilatte] received a letter from Mgr. Heycamp, Old Catholic Bishop of Utrecht urging him to break off with the Episcopal Church,' Queen, 35. Also interesting is the fact that Pruter offers no appropriate citation(s) in his book *History of the Old Catholic Church* to validate that such an event occurred either.

21   Pruter, *History of the Old Catholic Church,* 34.

22   *Id.*, 36. Moss provides us with very early evidence of the growing intimate relationship between the Episcopal church (USA) and the Union of Utrecht stating, "In 1880 Bishop Herzog [the first Old Catholic bishop of Switzerland from 1876-1924], accompanied by Bishop Henry Cotterill [bishop of the Scottish Episcopal Diocese of Edinburgh from

1872-1886], attended the General Convention of the American Episcopal Church. He communicated at the opening service, and assisted in administering the chalice. He also preached and gave confirmation in America, where he was welcomed by all parties in the Episcopal Church. The American [Episcopal] bishops unanimously passed a resolution repudiating the decrees of Trent and the Vatican and the dogma of the Immaculate Conception, and declaring that the Old Catholic consecrations by a single bishop were lawful in the circumstances" (Moss, 332).

23   *Ibid.*

24   For further details about this consecration, i.e. where, when, who, how, see Moss, p. 291.

25   Moss, 291-292.

26   *Id.*, 292.

27   *Ibid.*

28   Most notably Pruter and Queen maintain that Vilatte, as well as other wandering independent bishops apart from the Old Catholic apostolic succession, are indeed part of an Old Catholicism of a different type than that of the Union of Utrecht— see esp. Queen, pp. 27-28; NeSmith, pp. 23-25, esp. at p. 23 (middle paragraph); Pruter, *History of the Old Catholic Church,* 34-39; and Pruter, *The Old Catholic Sourcebook,* pp. 26-29—admittedly Pruter seems to be a bit more reasonable in his exposition on Vilatte than that of Queen's and NeSmith's rendition. However, their overall similar conclusions that

independent bishops consecrated in the Vilatte succession are Old Catholic is plainly an inaccurate interpretation of history.

29   See, Moss, p. 291-292.

30   This is a good example of how Old Catholics *qualitatively* (versus numerically) define the essence of a local church universal. According to Moss, Mathew was elected by the local church synod of England consisting of seventeen priests and sixteen lay members in union with the college of bishops of the Union of Utrecht (Moss, 300).

31   Moss, 301.

32   Moss, 298.

33   Although Mathew did adhere and put his signature to the Declaration of the Union of Utrecht before being consecrated an Old Catholic bishop for the local church of England.

34   It is interesting to note that Mathew was baptized a Roman Catholic as an infant to satisfy his father who was a Roman Catholic, and then was baptized again at age two in the Anglican church to satisfy his mother who was an Anglican (Moss, 298). Some might conclude that this vacillation between the two churches was instilled in him from a very early age.

35   See Moss, esp. pp. 300-301.

36   Moss informs us that "as early as 1896 an attempt was made to begin an Old Catholic movement in England, but it came to nothing, because the priest

proposed as bishop made his submission to Rome. In 1902 an *application* was made to the Dutch Old Catholic bishops to consecrate an English Old Catholic bishop. The candidate was the Rev. Richard O'Halloran, a Roman Catholic secular [diocesan] priest...who had quarreled with his superiors. O'Halloran asked Bishop Herzog [first Old Catholic bishop of Switzerland] to come and give confirmation at his church...He [Herzog] made inquiries, and advised great caution [to the Old Catholic college of bishops]: so nothing was done. In 1908 O'Halloran tried again, and this time the instrument of his purpose was Dr. Mathew." Moss, 298 (my italics).

37 Moss claims that Mathew was duped right along with the Union of Utrecht's college of bishops by O'Halloran stating, 'On his [Mathew] return to England, he found that the support which he had been led to expect did not exist. He [Mathew] afterwards declared that he had been grievously misled; he offered to retire, but the Dutch bishops refused his offer.' Moss, 301.

38 Moss, 300.

39 *Ibid.*

40 See Moss, 301.

41 Moss, 301.

42 The local Old Catholic church of Holland did not declare its acceptance of Anglican Holy Orders until 1925. See J. Robert Wright *Anglican and Old Catholic*

Theology Compared in *Old Catholics & Anglicans 1931-1981*, esp. p. 129 (bottom paragraph).

43   Moss, 301.

44   Moss, 301.

45   See Moss, p. 301-302.

46   Moss, 302.

47   See Moss, 303.

48   Moss, 304 (my italics).

49   See Moss, p. 304 (middle of the paragraph).

50   See Queen, p. xi (fourth and fifth paragraph in the *Forward* section).

51   Self-published authors like Queen misrepresent Mathew and Vilatte as being persecuted pioneers who battled the omnivorous Episcopal Church in America and the Union of Utrecht. This is plainly an irresponsible portrayal of these two men as well as the Episcopal and Union of Utrecht churches. See Queen, esp. pp. xi, 22-23; 30-42.

52   See Nesmith, 23.

53   This statement does not imply that both churches were immune from making other mistakes. As we will soon see, the Union of Utrecht was not immune from making more mistakes after the Vilatte and Mathew situations. This will become evident when we discuss in section two of this chapter the other history of Old Catholicism in the U.S.: the Polish National Catholic Church. What is implied by this statement is that both churches remained centered

in the grace of the Holy Spirit, even in the midst of the mistakes made, and learned from these situations by not mirroring them in the future.

54   Laurence Orzell, *Variations on an Old Catholic Theme: The Polish National Catholic Church* in *Old Catholics & Anglicans 1931-1981*, 40.

55   *Id.*, 41.

56   *Id.*, 42.

57   *Id.*, 45.

58   See the National Council of Churches Membership Statistics at http://www.ncccusa.org/news/061102 updatedstats.htm

59   Laurence J. Orzell, "Disunion of Utrecht: Old Catholics Fall Out over New Doctrines," *Touchstone: A Journal of Mere Christianity*, 2004 [magazine online]; available from http://www.touchstonemag.com/archives/article.php?id=17-04-056-r; Internet; accessed 6 October 2007.

60   Orzell clearly states that "...the principal cause of the split was the admission of women to the ministerial priesthood by several of the Old Catholic churches, the decision reflected longstanding tensions between the 'progressive' majority and the PNCC over other issues, such as homosexuality and ecumencism" (Orzell, *Disunion of Utrecht*, 1).

61   Grace, 4.

62   *Ibid.*

63 M. Edmund Hussey, "Nicholas Afanassiev's Eucharistic Ecclesiology: A Roman Catholic Viewpoint," *Journal of Ecumenical Studies,* vol. 12, no. 2 (1975): 237.

64 *Id.*, 241(my italics).

65 Grace, 5.

66 Plekon, 154.

67 Orzell, *Disunion of Utrecht,* 3.

68 Orzell, *Disunion of Utrecht,* 4.

69 Orzell clearly states, "Prime Bishop Nemkovich did not require much time to conclude that the term 'separation' actually meant 'divorce.' In an open letter to all PNCC clergy and laity he pointed out that 'contrary to the provisions of the IBC's 'Statute'....a majority decided...to remove the PNCC from the Union of Utrecht.' While expressing regret, he reminded the faithful that 'recent innovations adopted by the West European church have altered the character of the Utrecht Union to such an extent that it is no longer the same communion that Bishop Franciszek Hodur joined as a result of his consecration in 1907 (Orzell, *Disunion of Utrecht,* 4-5)." There is no doubt on either side that the PNCC refused to participate in full communion with the Union of Utrecht.

70 The Archbishop of Utrecht argued, "...that the PNCC could and should restore full communion even though it did not recognize Old Catholic female clergy. In other words, the touchstone of

what it meant to be 'Old Catholic' was to be in full communion rather than to share the same (confessional/denominational) beliefs in faith, order, and morals" (Orzell, *Disunion of Utrecht*, 4). Again, Orzell's confusion is in his assumption that the Old Catholics are working from a universal ecclesiology like the PNCC. It is lucidly clear from Orzell's statement here that the Old Catholics are working from a eucharistic rather than a universal ecclesiology.

71 Orzell, *Disunion of Utrecht*, 1.

72 The term "homosexual" appears no where in the original Koine Greek New Testament. Further, the word "homosexuality" defined as a loving and caring long-term relationship between two consenting same-sex adults was something altogether unknown in the early church—meaning, homosexuality is a modern concept unknown to those in the ancient world, except for the sexual act itself. The word "homosexual," if it exists in an English bible translation, is considered today by most prominent biblical scholars to be an inaccurate translation of the original Greek text.

73 The Declaration of Utrecht (1889), § 6.

74 Although closer ties to Rome are being publicly established with minor success.

75 See Queen, p. xi (fourth paragraph from the top).

76 Queen, xi (my italics).

77 Contemporary Roman Catholic theologians are not only influenced by the scholastic theological teach-

ings of Aquinas (among others in this period) and the later Council of Trent, but further assert that such teachings "…are significant building blocks…" for specific doctrinal teachings for the Roman Magisterium on theological topics like the Eucharist. For further reading on this subject see Irwin, *Models of the Eucharist*, pp. 187-90; 250-51.

78   See Pruter, *A History of the Old Catholic Church,* p. 65; and NeSmith, p. 24 (second full paragraph).

79   Refer back to the previous chapter (chapter two) for the Union of Utrecht's definition of what constitutes a "local catholic church".

80   Richard Giles, *Creating Uncommon Worship: Transforming the Liturgy of the Eucharist* (Collegeville, MN: Liturgical Press), 75.

81   A French term used to imply that with power and prestige there is an equal social accountability and responsibility.

82   See John D. Zizioulas, *Eucharist, Bishop, Church: The Unity of the Church in the Divine Eucharist and the Bishop during the First Three Centuries*, trans. Elizabeth Theokritoff (Brookline, MA: Holy Cross Orthodox Press 2001), esp. pp. 87-106.

83   See James Monroe Barnett, *The Diaconate: A Full and Equal Order* (Valley Forge, PA: Trinity Press International, 1995), esp. pp. 36-40.

84   See Zizioulas, *Eucharist, Bishop, Church: The Unity of the Church in the Divine Eucharist and the Bishop during the First Three Centuries*, esp. pp. 200-204.

85   See Zizioulas, *Eucharist, Bishop, Church*, esp. p. 197.

86   For further study and research on the episcopacy, ministerial priesthood and Eucharist in the church of the first three-centuries, see Zizioulas, *Eucharist, Bishop, Church: The Unity of the Church in the Divine Eucharist and the Bishop during the First Three Centuries*, esp. pp. 197-98.

87   Barnett asserts that "It was the gradual rise of clericalism in the Medieval Church that resulted in the ministry coming to be considered the possession of the clergy [ordained priesthood]. The inevitable consequence is the Church's impoverishment of the gifts the Spirit has given to all the baptized. Ministry is sorely limited by the relatively small number of clergy and is usually exercised largely in terms of serving the internal needs of the institution [of the Church]." Barnett, 166.

88   I am aware that clericalism is alive and well not just in the Roman Catholic Church, but also in other Christian denominations. I single out the Roman church here because it is the context to which Old Catholicism was born out of, and is a church that fosters an embedded identity of ontological difference between the clergy and laity. Barnett supports my above assertion stating, "Richard Rashke reports that 80 percent of American Roman Catholic priests believe there is an ontological difference between clergy and laity." Barnett, 167.

89   Zizioulas, *Eucharist, Bishop, Church*, 202.

90   See Aebersold, 87.

91   Ploeger, 21.

92   Jesus himself testifies in John 6:37-40 that only
      through his personhood does one have life, and that
      both scripture and tradition points not to life itself,
      but to him who is life and communion with God
      the Father. See also Jesus' "vine and branches" dis-
      course in John 15.

93   The sacramental priestly ministry that describes
      Holy Order and its equal ranks is part of the one
      priesthood of Christ that is shared by all the bap-
      tized. Holy Order ranks are equal to that of the
      priesthood of the baptized, but its *charismata* (gifts
      of the Spirit) serves the local body differently from
      the *charismata* of the laity, which is to emphasize
      that the term *difference* does not necessarily connote
      a hierarchal rank per se. This is true also for the
      three ranks in the sacrament of Holy Order.
      Meaning, all three ranks of Holy Order are different
      yet related to each other in their differences through
      the shared *indelible charisma* of communion found
      in the one person of the local bishop who repre-
      sents Christ in the totality of what is Eucharist with
      the local body of Christ in communion with other
      local-universal churches throughout the world.
      Barnett attests to this equality found in the three
      ranks of ministry stating, "As the ancient councils
      and many of the fathers of the early Church saw, it
      was good for one to demonstrate by service in the
      Church proper qualifications for positions of lead-
      ership entailing greater responsibility, particularly
      in reference to the episcopate. However, to see the

ministry of the Church essentially as a graded succession of offices not only contradicts the organic character with which the Church was originally endowed by Christ and his Spirit but also affirms the very worldliness denied by Christ. Such a view sees the ministry largely in terms of authority, power, and honor, not of service. The ministry (of Holy Order) is properly *diakonia*, service, a truth needing reiteration just because it has been so neglected, if not forgotten." Barnett, 143.

94   Zizioulas, *Being as Communion,* 227.

95   Zizioulas provides an insightful exegesis on Paul's canticle of love in 1 Cor. 13 as an expression "…of his theology of the *charismata* in the previous chapter (1 Cor. 12)." See Zizioulas, *Being as Communion*, esp. p. 227 at footnote no. 48. See also Christ's great commandment to his disciples, "I give you a new commandment: love one another. As I have loved you, so you also should love one another (John 13:34); and the evangelist has Christ repeat this great commandment later in John 15:17 to emphasize its importance as being disciples of the *Way*.

96   Aidan Kavanagh, *Elements of Rite: A Handbook of Liturgical Style* (New York: Pueblo Publishing Co., 1982), 38.

97   The viability of any church parish has little to do how many members are 'listed in its roster,' and has more to do with the qualitative vitality of its liturgical and missional life together as members of the local body of Christ.

98   See Pruter, *A History of the Old Catholic Church*, esp. p. 73.

CHAPTER FOUR

1   See Moss, p. 350 (second full paragraph).

2   Moss, 318-19; see also Huelin, *Old Catholics and Ecumenism* in *Old Catholics & Anglicans*, p. 141.

3   According to Moss, there are five periods which define Old Catholic and Anglican relations that lead up to the Bonn Agreement of 1931. For further reading see Moss, pp. 330-339.

4   Moss provides us with but one example of this kind of sentiment in his book when he quotes from a letter written by an Anglican theologian, J.M. Neale, concerning his foundational work and research of the church of Utrecht in 1851 stating: 'It is impossible to close my task without wishing for the knowledge of a prophet as to the future fate of that communion [Utrecht]...It seems to me that the little remnant of this afflicted Church are reserved for happier days. Wherever and whenever that Ecumenical Council may be, or whatever other means God shall employ to restore the lost unity of Christendom, the labours, and trials, and sufferings of this communion will not be forgotten' (Moss, 331).

5   See Afanassieff's essay "The Church Which Presides in Love," in *The Primacy of Peter*, esp. p. 71-73.

6   Moss, 327.

7   *Ibid.*

8   Moss quotes Bishop Josef Hubert Reinkens' (first
     Old Catholic bishop of Germany from 1873-1896)
     pastoral letter written in 1881 to his diocese
     "...express[ing] his joy in the [Anglican] services he
     had attended...and said: 'Every Catholic who is not
     so unhistorically narrow as to recognize only his
     own Mass, must feel himself at home also in the
     Anglican celebration of the Holy Communion—
     must feel borne along by the Catholic spirit' (Moss,
     333).

9   J. Robert Wright, *Anglican and Old Catholic Theology
     Compared* in *Old Catholics & Anglicans*, 125.

10   See "Appendix B."

11   Anglican theologian, J. Robert Wright, writing in
     the early 1980's asserts that these points of agree-
     ment are relevant in the contemporary church
     because Old Catholic and Anglican theologians
     continue to reference them in their work. I concur
     with Wright and believe the 1874 theological theses
     agreement will always hold relevance as being the
     preliminary instrument that paved the way toward
     the full communion which was realized at Bonn in
     1931. See Wright, p. 125 (middle of second full
     paragraph). Moreover, I believe the 1874 theologi-
     cal theses agreement was instrumental in helping to
     form the Anglican "four principles of unity" resolu-
     tion at the Lambeth Conference of 1888. (See 1976
     Book of Common Prayer of the Episcopal Church
     (USA), p. 877-78).

12 *The Harpercollins Encyclopedia of Catholicism,* 1995 ed., s.v. "Ecumenical Councils."

13 Wright, 127.

14 See Moss, pp. 346-47; and Wright, p. 127 (first full paragraph).

15 The Church of Utrecht eventually recognized the unbroken historic episcopacy of the Anglican Communion in 1925, thus removing the last major stumbling block toward full communion between them. See Moss, p. 339 (middle full paragraph), and p. 340 (middle of second paragraph); see also Wright, p. 129 (bottom paragraph).

16 See Dwight Zscheile, "A More True 'Domestic and Foreign Missionary Society': Toward a Missional Polity for the Episcopal Church," *Journal of Religious Leadership* 5, vol. 1 & 2 (2006): esp. pp. 8-11; see also Wright, pp. 127-28.

17 See Wright, p. 127-28; see also Paul Avis, *The Identity of Anglicanism: Essentials of Anglican Ecclesiology,* pp. 81-117.

18 Moss, 342.

19 Moss, 345-46.

20 See the 1931 Bonn Agreement in Appendix C.

21 Zizioulas, *Eucharist, Bishop, Church,* 114-15 (my italics).

22 Runcie, *Old Catholics & Anglicans,* 2. See also, Urs von Arx, *Unity and Communion, Mystical and Visible* in *Towards Further Convergence: Anglican and Old*

Catholic Ecclesiologies, esp. pp. 163-64 (starting at the bottom paragraph on p. 163).

23   See Wright, p. 130.

24   Runcie, 3.

25   Runcie, 3.

26   Zizioulas, *Being as Communion*, 257.

27   See Zizioulas, *Being as Communion*, p. 258.

28   See Zizioulas, *Being as Communion*, p. 259-60.

29   Runcie, 4.

30   Zizioulas, *Being as Communion*, 259.

31   See Runcie, p. 5.

32   This is why I relate so well to Mark's ending the gospel claiming that the women who had seen the resurrected Jesus "...fled from the tomb, for terror and amazement had seized them: and they said nothing to anyone, for they were afraid." (Mark 16:8) Resurrection is radical and shocking. Of course fear and amazement will be part of this experience, but we (like the women in Mark's gospel) must eventually move beyond our fears to see the joy and life-giving communion this kind of transformation offers us. Nobody was ever the same after Christ's resurrection; they were changed for the better.   So it is the case with the Anglicans and Old Catholics as they continue the path towards fully living out the eucharistic nature of communion the Bonn Agreement sets before them.

33   Moss, 350.

CHAPTER FIVE

1   Urs von Arx, *Unity and Communion, Mystical and Visible* in *Towards Further Convergence: Anglican and Old Catholic Ecclesiologies*, 168.

2   See the Philadelphia Episcopal Cathedral's website: http://www.philadelphiacathedral.org/; Episcopal Diocese of San Francisco communities, i.e. St. Cuthbert's: http://www.stcuthbertsoakland.org/; and St. Gregory of Nyssa: http://www.saintgregorys.org/

APPENDICES

1 See Moss, p. 348.

LaVergne, TN USA
17 February 2010
173440LV00001B/15/P